Coming to My Senses

Coming to My Senses

One Woman's Cochlear Implant Journey

CLAIRE H. BLATCHFORD

Gallaudet University Press
Washington, DC

Gallaudet University Press
Washington, DC 20002
http://gupress.gallaudet.edu

Library of Congress Cataloging-in-Publication Data

Blatchford, Claire H.

Coming to my senses : one woman's cochlear implant journey / Claire H. Blatchford.

pages   cm

ISBN 978-1-56368-615-3 (pbk. : alk. paper) — ISBN 1-56368-615-5 (pbk.) —

ISBN 978-1-56368-616-0 (e-book) — ISBN 1-56368-616-3 (e-book)

1. Blatchford, Claire H.—Health.

2. Cochlear implants—Patients—United States—Biography.   I. Title.

RF305.B53 2014

617.8'9092—dc23

[B]

2014014543

Contents

Introduction

TEN DAYS after turning six, I became profoundly deaf in both ears overnight from the mumps. Imagine your hearing being switched off with one quick flick of fate. There was no hearing aid powerful enough for my use in the early 1950s, but my parents chose what is referred to as the "oral" approach to communication. They expected me to learn how to speechread and to continue to speak orally rather than learn American Sign Language (also known as ASL). They chose this approach because they wanted me to remain in the hearing world, so when I recovered, I returned to the public school classroom I'd been in. There must have been some plan at school, but I was never aware of it, as there were no Individualized Education Programs at that time. Apart from my paternal grandmother, who had a progressive hearing loss later in life, and the hard of hearing headmistress at the high school I attended, I did not meet other deaf people my age until I was twenty-three.

When I got my first hearing aid at twelve, two things became evident. The first was that I could only use an aid in one ear, my right ear. When I tried repeatedly to use one in my left ear I got extreme vertigo and stomach upset. This is still the case. So my left ear "retired" early on!

The other thing was that sound, as I heard it through the hearing aid in my right ear, did not sound at all as I remember. In fact, it hurt! In six years I had lost touch with sounds from the world. This was a crucial moment. If I hadn't been pushed and cajoled back then to move beyond the pain, embarrassment, and frustration of learning to hear with a hearing aid, I don't know where I'd be now. It's highly likely this book would never have been written.

I progressed from one hearing aid to another as the technology developed and my appetite for hearing grew. What I was getting through the hearing aid, though, was always supplemental rather than primary. I depended on speechreading, and no matter how hard I worked at that—and I still depend on it—there were always stumbling blocks and gaps in my understanding. For one thing you may not know who is speaking, and the more people there are participating in a conversation the harder it becomes, nor can you always see a person's face, and everybody speaks differently. Some hardly move their lips, while, at the other end of the spectrum, are those who over-enunciate, unknowingly making it harder. When you depend on speechreading, you are constantly playing a guessing game. If you get five words out of eight—and I'll be talking more about this later—you have to piece things together quickly. The solicitousness of the over-enunciator slows this up considerably. One doesn't have to get *every single word* in a sentence to understand what's being communicated, yet hearing people often seem to think that's necessary and labor on.

At age six I just wanted to keep going, and I didn't reflect on the how of understanding people. I was speechreading, face reading, body reading, and reading every situation I landed in long before I learned to read and write in first grade. At twelve, when I finally learned to make use of it, the hearing aid enabled me to become aware of other important factors. These were the presence of others via sound—such as the dog barking in another room—and some sense of volume. When my mother said, "Shhh . . . ," I began to connect that to my own shouting and would lower my voice.

With each new hearing aid I was able to inch my way back a bit into hearing, but there was no question that I was "hearing" primarily through my eyes rather than the hearing aid in my right ear. My elementary and high school years were not exactly easy, as you'll see in the pages ahead. But as you'll also see, there were surprises and plenty of discoveries along the way.

When I first heard about and did research on the cochlear implant over twenty years ago, I was in my forties, and I shied away from it. (For those who are not familiar with the cochlear implant—what it is, how it is inserted surgically, and how it works—you might want first to read the appendix at the end of this book by Jeanne Coburn, my audiologist.) The technology was not as advanced as it is today; back then I felt I had found my way and was not about to endanger the balance I had won over several decades.

Then, at age sixty-six, I changed my mind. Outwardly this change of mind was sudden. Inwardly, I now see, several factors were pointing me in that direction. A major shift occurred when it became obvious to me as a teacher of the deaf that the children who had cochlear implants responded far more quickly, both in class and in mainstream situations, than the children who used hearing aids. For example, we would be at a drive-in ordering ice cream, and the children with implants always heard when their order was filled and how much it cost. Those with hearing aids, including myself, had to keep an eye on the window and often misinterpreted what was said. Who doesn't want to know when her ice cream is ready? Who wants to make a fool of herself in simple everyday exchanges? This change in my view of the cochlear implant (CI) for myself, and the changes it set in motion after I got it—which are still reverberating throughout my life—lie at the heart of the journey I have to share with you.

Before I went into surgery for the CI, I began writing about it in my journal: the pros and cons, my hopes and fears, my observations about the process, conversations with others around it, and more. Journaling has always enabled me to better understand myself and the world around me. My father, who began his work life as a newspaper reporter and became a banker, told me when I first learned to write, "Maybe you can't hear, but you can write." I heard and followed this encouragement (my father also gave me my first journal—to this day blank notebook pages fill me with a sense of anticipation and excitement), and over many years I discovered that putting experiences down on paper in words often made them clearer and more real. In addition, maybe I couldn't hear my own words when I spoke them, but I could hear them loud and strong when I *wrote* them!

As a child it was a great relief to be able to sound off in my journal—which I hid under my mattress! Many were the pages I filled with comments like "Damn math!" or "I hate, hate, HATE speech therapy!" There were also first crushes, stirrings of spiritual sensibilities, and flashes of joy, much of which came out in poetry. At age eleven I knew I wanted to be a writer. I have had twenty-one books and numerous stories and articles published. Some are listed at the end of this book.

It was natural for me to work through my thoughts and feelings about getting the cochlear implant on paper. After surgery I tried to catch in writing what was happening, even *as* it happened, and almost everything I wrote during those first twelve months was in verse. It is tempting here to start telling you what poetry means to me, but I will, and instead quote Mary Oliver: *Poetry is a life-cherishing force.*

During my first year with the implant I was brimming over with amazement, wonder, and gratitude. I was puzzled, too, and was always asking, "What's that sound? Who made it? Where's it coming from?" What is behind such questions if not life-cherishing forces? As I grew accustomed to this new form of hearing, I wrote less poetry and switched back to prose, as other matters took center stage.

Before Thanksgiving of the year I received the implant, I went through my journal and gathered many of the poems together in chronological order to share with family and friends. Several said they wanted "more." "More what?" I wondered. "More about how it has changed your life," emailed one friend. Another wrote that the poems "begged" to be expanded upon. When asked what he meant, he said he thought the poems were too bare by themselves. My response: "I don't think this group of poems is supposed to be an autobiography." Yet I had understood what he was suggesting, and I sat down and began writing.

As I attempted to describe my new experiences with sound, I couldn't help but reflect on my life journey with deafness. Furthermore, as I wrote, I felt myself, even at age sixty-seven, discovering and rediscovering not only hearing, and hearing through my eyes, but the interweaving of *all* the physical senses as guides to understanding the world.

This journey continues. I can't perceive an end to it as long as I'm here on the earth, alive and wondering. Come join me, beginning with the acute ambivalence I experienced before deciding to get the cochlear implant.

The Inner Debate

Do I make do
with what I am,
where I am,
what life has brought me
or
stick my face
in God's face
beg, plead, insist
on more
or better?

For over sixty years
I've found my way
through deafness,
forged a philosophy:
the way's there
when the will's there,
help *is* there
answers *are* there
to be found—
always!
I've done a pretty good job.
No one's complaining.
Why change course now?
Having learned how to use it

why toss out the hearing aid?
Why start all over?

  Dare to let go of what you've achieved.
  Dare to open to change.
  Deafness doesn't belong
  to any person
  or group of people.
  What's right for one
  doesn't make other approaches wrong.
  Let deafness
  go on showing you
  there's no end
  to what can be discovered
  of hearing,
  listening,
  being human.

I've been lucky:
tough-love parents,
inspired teachers, true friends,
opportunities—
always enough,
sometimes more than enough—
above all
life in a free world
where the deaf are not
despised, scorned, cast out—
why should I ask for more?
  Why *not* ask for more?
  Why not *want* more?

I'm scared.
I don't want
someone cutting into my head . . .

❧

"WHY," people have asked, "would there be any question or debate about getting a cochlear implant?"

They are, I guess, assuming that all people want to hear in the same way they hear. Furthermore, isn't the world primarily a hearing world? Don't people who talk greatly outnumber the deaf who use sign language? Yes, it makes sense. From their perspective the cochlear implant represents a chance to be "normal." They are also assuming that the cochlear implant can "restore" hearing. This, for me at least, has not happened and probably won't happen. It's not just that when I take the implant off I am profoundly deaf, it's that what I hear by way of the implant sounds "electronic" and incomplete compared to what you hear. And the part of my brain that processes sounds may never again be as agile as it was before I lost my hearing at six.

After I got the implant, a deaf friend asked a different "Why?" question. She's a lovely person, a dozen years younger than me. She speaks and signs, uses one hearing aid, works in the hearing world, and is most comfortable among other deaf people. I'll never forget the look of horror on her face when she caught sight of the implant processor and the magnet attached to my head. "I don't believe what I'm seeing!" she signed as she spoke. "*Why* did you get it?"

She made me feel like a defector.

From her perspective I was trying to be what I'm not: a hearing person. She believes deaf people have their own unique experiences, culture, and ways of communicating. If you take the time to look at it through her eyes, her view makes sense. Differences should be observed, respected, honored, and celebrated. Trying to make profoundly deaf people hear and behave like hearing people doesn't make sense. There are always going to be differences. Likewise, it doesn't make sense for the profoundly deaf person with a cochlear implant to think she is now a hearing person. Why deny what one is?

I was actually *not* thinking about either of these perspectives during my inner debate. The closest I came to it was when I thought about my family: my husband, our daughters, their husbands, and our grandchildren. They all have normal hearing and have always known me as a deaf person. For them, it's part of who I am. None of them were pushing for me to get the implant. But I *did* wonder, as I've wondered many times throughout my life, wouldn't it be a whole lot easier for them if I could hear? If it was possible, I certainly wanted to make it easier for them.

And would it be a whole lot easier for me? Like my family, I, too, have always known myself as a deaf person. Deafness has always been there to push against, respond to, and work with. When my ability to understand what people are saying is limited, there must be other ways to understand them. Turns out, as I said in my poem, there *always* are other ways.

In short, I was comfortable in the relationship I'd developed with deafness—not as a condition I happened to land in—but as my teacher. The lessons it has brought me have gone way beyond needing to find other ways of hearing. The lessons have been about learning, not just to hear, but to listen, and not just with my physical body and all the amazing technological assistance available today, but also with my soul and my spirit.

So I wasn't looking for a way to escape the condition. It was the thought of rocking the boat after a lifetime of learning how to travel in it that got me debating. The sailing was smooth, why change course? It's one thing to talk about learning to listen, and quite another to offer your head up to the surgeon's knife, trusting that it will enhance the listening process.

The First Lesson

I was in the hospital. It was about a week after I'd lost my hearing, and the nurses insisted I sit in a wheelchair. As I couldn't hear their reasons for this (or anything else), they had to use physical force to make me comply. It was my ears, not my legs, that were the problem, and I was itching to run, sled, and play in the January snow.

The day before I was released, I was taken in my bathrobe in the wheelchair up several floors and down the hall to a door with a small rectangular window above the doorknob. I could see the glass but was too low down to be able to look through it.

The nurse knocked before wheeling me into the room. It was full of men dressed in white—doctors or medical students— seated, facing another man, also in white, behind a podium. The nurse parked me beside the podium, facing the audience, and went to the back of the room.

I understood, from the way everybody was looking at me, that the man was talking about me. I hoped they weren't going to tie me down again on the table in the bare, windowless room. When I was first admitted to the hospital, they'd tried, unsuccessfully, to give me a spinal tap. Unable to understand anything that was said, terrified of the long needle and the red fluid in the syringe, I fought them off. Not even my mother could make me calm down, and I needed to be awake in order for the spinal tap to be effective. (It may not have been feasible or safe then to sedate me.) Learning to read written words and learning to read lips would come later.

Suddenly the man leaned toward me holding a pencil in one hand level to my eyes. I looked past the pencil at him and concluded, from the expression on his face, he was asking me to identify the object in his hand.

Of course it was a pencil! Did he really think I didn't know what a pencil was?

Insulted, I looked past him, across the room and out the window. I felt hot, flustered, and embarrassed. I didn't like being on display in a room full of strangers in my bathrobe.

Minutes later the nurse turned my chair and began wheeling me out.

As we were departing a question flashed through my mind, "Does he think I'm stupid?"

I needed to tell the man it *was* a pencil he'd held before me. But we were already on our way out the door.

"It's a pencil! It's a pencil!" I exclaimed trying to get up.

The nurse pushed me back down, held me down, and went on wheeling. But not before I'd peered through the tiny glass window.

The man was looking at his audience. I'd missed my chance to tell him it was a pencil.

I was too young to be able to describe to anyone—including myself—what I learned in that moment. I'm a slow learner in that I often don't understand experiences I've had until much later. Sometimes, decades later. But I remember the experiences, usually vividly, and can remember the feelings that came with them.

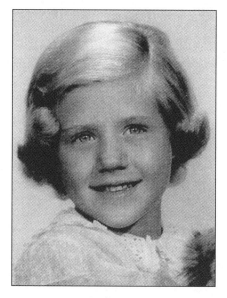

Early years.

The dominant feeling then was anxiety. Everyone was trying to communicate with me in the way they thought would work best: pointing, tapping my arm, squeezing my hands, drawing pictures, turning my head to look at their faces, making exaggerated facial expressions, and more. The thread that sews us all together—language—had, for me, been cut. So there I was careening around, grasping at different bits of threads, trying to make sense of the world. And the first thing I picked up was the way people looked at me. Their faces told me I was damaged. I knew my ears were damaged, yet their faces were wondering about more than my ears. The doctor with the pencil forced it into my consciousness: people were wondering whether my mind had also been damaged. Had I become stupid? "Stupid" was the warning word from my parents when my brother and I did silly things.

I knew right then, with all of my six-year-old being, that my mind was fine. Maybe I'd been acting up a bit, *had* been silly throwing tantrums, but I'd understood that the doctor wanted me to identify the pencil and—I hadn't done it. Had he concluded I was stupid? Or, as people said then, "deaf and dumb"?

The anxiety propelled me forward, toward speechreading, reading, talking, finding the thread any way I could. I felt an urgent need to make it clear to the world that inside, in my mind, I was intact. Even now, when I don't get something and see the "What's the matter with her?" look on the face of a stranger, I sense a distant edge, a prick, a whiff, of the anxiety I felt that day over sixty years ago.

Moment of Decision

My one hearing aid was faltering:
loud-soft, off-on.
The tight spot in my neck was getting tighter
as I strained to catch with my eyes
what I couldn't get through the aid.

After the hearing test Barbara said,
"Your hearing's worse."

I laughed.
"I've been profoundly deaf since six,
what's after profound?"

"Cosmic deafness."

I thought she was kidding, but her face was serious.
I'd become as deaf as deaf can be—
that is, when you're talking about it scientifically.
Inside I could still hear thoughts, feelings,
voices, singing, music,
words rising up off pages,
the earth breathing into my toes.

But outside
to the world—

this world—
I was off in space.

"There's no hearing aid that's going to help you,
only the cochlear implant."

"I'm scared."
There—finally—I'd said it out loud.

She nodded.

If I got the implant
there would be no going back to the hearing aid,
dizzy spells might worsen,
tinnitus, facial paralysis, loss of taste, headaches—
all were possibilities.
My right ear,
my more alert,
more awake ear,
would have to be the one,
the left ear was too far gone.

The biggest question yet:
would my brain be able to move
from a trickle to a torrent of noise?
Would sounds be torment or treasure?

Barbara guessed my thoughts.
"The implant's come a long way."

I'd explored the possibility twenty years earlier.

My gut said no.
Later I knew that was the right decision—
only seven of the fifteen operations by that surgeon
had been successful.

Barbara waited.

"Give me a surefire reason to get it."

She didn't skip a beat.
"Now your eyes do 95 percent of the work,
the hearing aid 5 percent—sometimes less.
With the implant it would be more like fifty-fifty,
your eyes and your right ear."

My dear eyes!
My most faithful friends!
Once I experienced blindness for three days
because of an accident,
and learned I'm no Helen Keller.

It was time to protect and thank those eyes.

With that realization a cascade of other reasons rushed out:

It was time to step into the world of technology
many of the deaf children I worked with inhabited.

It was time to try meeting my hearing family on their turf.

It was time to hear what I hadn't heard since I was six:
wind, rain, rivers, crickets. . . .

THE MOMENT when I knew, "I'm going to get it!" stands out vividly in my memory.

It was a sweltering August day. Barbara, mentioned in the poem above, was my audiologist. After I left her office, I sat in the air-conditioned car in the parking lot for a couple of minutes, marveling at the fact that I'd just said "Yes!" to something I'd been saying "No!" to for at least twenty years. I recall craving a Coke or a chocolate bar—as though, physically, I'd completed a marathon and needed a pickup—but not stopping to get either on the way home because I was in a hurry to share the news with Ed.

The decision *felt* right, that's all I knew. It felt right in my mind and in my heart and now it felt right in my gut too.

For years I'd given others, including my coworkers at Clarke Schools for Hearing and Speech where I worked, coherent reasons for *not* getting the implant. All the reasons I have already stated here: I was doing okay (they always nodded in agreement when I said this), and if the implant didn't work, I wouldn't be able to go back to a hearing aid because the sixteen thousand hair cells in my cochlea would be destroyed when the twenty-two electrodes were embedded in it, and to hear with a hearing aid you need those hair cells. Concrete facts of this sort can be tremendously reassuring, like bodyguards in a circle around you.

But . . .

The word "but" simply wouldn't leave me alone.

But what about your eyes? The experience with near blindness, which I mention in the last poem, was terrifying. It was an extremely windy day and a sharp object flew into my left eye, ripping the cornea. I had to have surgery. The pain was acute. I needed to stay in a darkened room, could not open my left eye, and my right eye teared up constantly. For almost three days I was unable to see clearly or to read faces, lips, emails, handwritten notes, books, the newspaper, anything. Communication, even with my husband, was reduced, for the most part, to my asking questions, then listening carefully for yes-or-no answers. Though I knew my eye would eventually heal and I'd be able to see again, I also knew my mother had suffered from severe macular degeneration and my father had had to have surgery twice for glaucoma. Oh boy, was I was going to be a chip off the old block? Would I be inheriting the same eye conditions? Yikes!

But what about your grandchildren—you'd like to be able to hear them, wouldn't you?

But what about your students with implants—you've even seen some of them talking on cell phones?

And so on.

These *buts* were not huge, they were not a matter of life or death, but they were persistent, especially the one involving my eyes. Apart from needing, as a deaf person, to be able to see in order to hear, I love looking at the world. There is always so much to see! Sometimes I feel I am, literally, eating and tasting the world through my eyes! My mother was an artist and was often doing watercolors on the kitchen table when I came home from school, and I'm sure this contributed to my appreciation both for art and for the natural world. Many of our conversations—hers and mine—were not spoken verbally, they arose out of this shared love of beauty. She would often ask me to pick a few flowers from a neighbor's garden for her to paint, would point at them when we were in the car. So I developed an eye early on for contrasting shapes and colors and, in the process, became an expert flower thief!

It's amazing how quickly I traveled beyond the other concerns surrounding the cochlear implant—the possibility of facial paralysis, or loss of taste, or increased dizziness, which I have always been prone to—through the power of having made a decision. I was no longer scared. I actually felt exhilarated. Sure, I'd get the jitters, and I'd have to meet with the doctor and get his take on it, sign my head over to his expertise, have an MRI, see about insurance coverage, figure out when it could be done, and so on. More important, there would be family and friends to go over the details with. But, for me, the course had been set, and I gave myself to it. I not only trusted the surgeon, the technology, the audiologist I'd be working with, the love of my husband, the support of my family and friends, the recuperative powers of the body, and the creative and educative forces within the brain, I also trusted that I would be protected and guided. If I was *not* meant to get the cochlear implant, I believed outer events or forces would interfere.

Amen!

I can't remember who taught me to pray back then, or if anyone suggested I pray, but pray I did when six years old. And hard! In the dark, on my knees by the side of the bed every evening after my parents had tucked me in, I told God I wanted my hearing back. I explained he had one week to turn the switch on again. At the end of the week, still unable to hear, I gave him another week. Then another. I figured he must be pretty busy.

Eventually, tired of repeating myself, I began asking, instead, for wings. If I couldn't get my hearing back, I wanted to fly.

Family portrait. I think I was four years old.

No wings sprouted on my shoulders, but I flew often in my dreams. When I was seven or eight, I dreamt almost nightly of becoming a bird, sometimes an owl, other times a parakeet. I'd circle over the classroom and would alight on the shoulder of the handsomest boy. I could poop on the heads of the mean girls too! Or, when going down the stairs behind my mother, my legs would suddenly stream out, straight behind, flat against my tummy, the legs of a goose in flight. If my mother turned around, I was instantly a girl again, upright on my feet, going demurely down the stairs. I could also hear perfectly in my dreams, which is still the case today. In fact, people don't even have to open their mouths to say what they mean, I "hear" and understand them perfectly. And they "hear" me perfectly as well.

"How charming!" you might say.

I believe every prayer sent straight from the heart *is* answered. Maybe not as expected or hoped, and often not as quickly as one wants. But, I've found that when I pay attention, and look and listen carefully, the answers come, or are, quite simply, there. And often they keep coming, keep appearing, for there may be more than one response to a request or a question. That six-year-old praying to God to turn her hearing back on didn't know a thing about the inventions and other forms of hearing help that would someday appear on her horizon: hearing aids, text telephones for the deaf, closed captioning, interpreters, oral transliterators, email, texting, the cochlear implant.

This has been the story of my life: there are *many* ways to hear. What I do with it, the listening part of it, is up to me. I suspect it was God himself who nudged me toward the decision to have the cochlear implant. He blew away every carefully crafted objection, made me hungry to connect in yet more ways with his world, gave my heart the needed courage.

It was as if God said, "Remember when you asked me to switch your hearing back on? Okay, now we're going to get literal about that. . . ."

Surgery and a Few Days After

There was nothing to do
but let go
of the fears
and
the hopes—
become a lone
papery white leaf
on a stream,
flowing who knows where.

My love stayed behind
in another room.
The surgeon met me
as I came down the hall
on the gurney,
an impish smile
in his brown eyes.
The mask was stretched tight
below his mouth
hiding his chin.
Another cloth was stretched tight
over his head
hiding his hair.
A single word formed on his lips,
"Ready?"

I nodded.

Now—
big gulp—
there's a magnet
inside my head!

Are paper clips,
screwdrivers and flashlights
going to come chasing
after me?

Am I going to be pulled
smack up
against the refrigerator
every time I pass it?

What about other people
with their magnets—
are we all going to huddle together
head to head?

What if all hell breaks loose
when I go through
a metal detector?
Is that why the doctor was smiling?

YES, INDEED, there is a magnet inside my head. If you
were with me, you could feel it with the tips of your

fingers, behind the uppermost lobe of my right ear, just under my skin. I *have* worried about its wandering around to some other place in my brain or the skin over it being worn away so that it's exposed. The imagination clearly likes flirting with possibilities of *every* sort, both wonderful and terrifying.

This magnet is attached to the internal part of the implant threaded through my cochlea. The outer part of the implant, the sound processor, is also attached to a magnet. When the sound processor is turned on and placed over my ear, the two magnets, outer and inner, click together, and the channel for sound opens up. Outer sounds are converted by the processor into electrical impulses, which are in turn delivered to my auditory nerve by way of the twenty-two electrodes in my cochlea.

I know that having a magnet inside my head is no big deal in these times. Screws, rods, bone replacements, transplanted organs, and more are now commonplace. Yet what I "hear" whenever I touch that spot where the inner magnet resides is this: I must live my life with wonder and gratitude. I must not take any of these gifts for granted and let them become assumed, expected, commonplace. Wonder and gratitude—not sound alone—are the magnets that draw the possibilities, the connections, and the rainbow of threads into and through my life.

And why do I say, "I must"? Because of the man with leprosy. I cannot, *must* not, forget him.

❧

The Second Lesson

My family moved to Tangiers, Morocco, for a year when I was eight. My father was working in international banking. It was a magical year. My brother and I attended an American school, and I had daily sessions with an American speech and hearing therapist who "just happened" to be there then too.

It was through this therapist that my mother heard about a faith healer. She was determined to take me to him with the hope that he could do something about my deafness. So one day the four of us, and the dog, drove to Casablanca.

Halfway there we stopped at a beach to picnic. It was an incredible beach for finding seashells, and soon my pockets, and my brother's pockets as well, were bulging with treasures.

Then suddenly my brother was pulling at my arm. My father, standing about twenty-five feet inland beside the car, was gesturing for us to come right away.

As we, and the dog, ran toward him, I saw my mother already in the car and a strange-looking figure standing not far from my father. It was a man with extreme leprosy. Bony, bent over, half-naked, his beard and hair a tangled thicket, one eye nothing but a white bulging mass, he could, for all I knew have been eighteen, thirty, or fifty years old. I had seen many beggars in Tangiers, but none this disfigured.

My brother and the dog clambered into the backseat. My father, both holding the door open and guarding it, pushed me in after them and slammed the door shut.

I looked out the window at the man. His hands were outstretched, his one good eye looked directly at me imploringly. As the car began moving, I turned to look at him out the back window. I could not escape the look in that dark eye. Even long after we'd zoomed away and had left him behind, I felt his despair.

When we got to the house where the faith healer worked, we found a long line of people waiting to see him. Most had leprosy, but we, the foreigners, were whisked right through the door.

My mother told me years later the faith healer told her he couldn't do anything about my deafness, but he could help her be more patient as a mother. She said he did help her. As for me, I knew that day that my hearing loss was *nothing* compared to the needs of the man with leprosy. Beside him I was whole.

Again, I understood I was fine.

No sounds from outside
for one week,
only my eyes
to connect me
with the world.

The fruits of sixty-one years
of reading lips, faces,
gestures, movements
were there for the picking.
I, the seasoned gardener,

sat on the sofa,
head wrapped in a turban,
communing with my six-year-old self.
I felt anew her puzzlement,
her need to keep moving

and the pervading sense
of severance.
Together we remembered how it had snowed
back then too:
thick, wet, slow, swirling flakes.

Snow and deafness have always been intertwined in my memory. The "blanket" quality of heavy snow makes me associate it with silence. Here is another snow poem I wrote over thirty years ago:

THE DEAF GIRL: A MEMORY

Once as a child I heard Prokofiev
On a record given to me.
I played it all the afternoons,
Wolves followed Peter through my rooms,
Forests and snow lay about me.
And then, as if to seal the spell,
I woke one morning and could not tell
Where in the silence of my room
The wolves waited.

         The snow waited
To melt. The forest did not stir.
Peter had disappeared. Frozen
In sunlight and shadows I've lived
With ears in my eyes, eyes in my heart.
Sometimes it seems that I have heard
Peter's footsteps in my heartbeat.
Sometimes I think I've seen
The wolves passing there.

Activation and Shortly After

H AD I GOTTEN my cochlear implant twenty years ago, I likely would have had to wait a month before it was turned on, or "activated," as they call it. Much more time was given then to the healing of the head wound. My wait in January of 2011 was for only one week. There was swelling but little to no pain. Nor had my head been shaved, at least not in any noticeable way.

I did not know what to expect. My history of learning to hear with amplification was, at the start, quite rocky. To repeat several things mentioned earlier: there was nothing powerful enough for my use when I was six years old. My father took me from doctor to doctor and dealer to dealer. Finally, when I was twelve, I got my first hearing aid, a box, about three inches by five in size, which, to my mortification, I had to wear strapped to my chest. In fact, my mother had a special bra made for me and played up the fact that I was on my way to becoming a woman. Her joke that stuffing lemons into the bra too, one on either side of the hearing aid, might make my figure more eye catching didn't amuse me at all. My mother was French, which may explain her humor. To speak metaphorically, I did not, at that point, have a sense for turning lemons into lemonade!

My parents were very excited by "The Brick" (as I called it), but at first *everything* that came to me through it sounded horrible. The world was loud, shrill, senseless, invasive. Amplification and comprehension are two quite different things.

My parents, John and Nelda Howell, in the early 1950s.

This, in my opinion, is one of the most misunderstood aspects of hearing loss. Many people think that if they just talk louder, even to the point of shouting, the deaf or hard of hearing person will get what they're saying. Scientists today have a term for this condition when the brain can't sort through and make sense of sounds, or tune out some sounds in order to listen to others. The term is "brain deaf." After six years of inactivity, that part of my brain didn't have a clue as to what to do with all the noises coming to it through The Brick. I would secretly unplug the machine or take the batteries out, but it was pretty obvious to my family, teachers, and therapist when the aid was off, because I didn't respond if they shouted behind my back. In addition, the ear mold—they were hard in those days, today they're softer, much more pliable—made my ear raw.

But, gradually, I learned to make use of it and came to depend on it. It not only alerted me to specific sounds—like the barking dog mentioned earlier, which, in turn, could mean someone was at the door—it also helped me to monitor my voice, and to sense the movement of noises around me. For example, I couldn't, with it, follow what my family was talking about at the dinner table—speechreading was needed for that—but, with the aid, I might sense *who* was talking. So I'd look in that person's direction.

When I was twenty-four, I got my first behind-the-ear aid. It was quite a bit more powerful than The Brick. I drove home from the dealer's office worried the car was going to fall apart. I was hearing rattles I'd never been aware of before. After that I got a new behind-the-ear aid every seven or eight years, each one a bit stronger than the last one. And every time I got a new aid, there was a period of adjustment, in the same way it may take you a while to adjust to new shoes or new eyeglasses. Then, at sixty-six, there was the dramatic decline in my hearing when my audiologist informed me no hearing aid would enable me to reach the level of sound I needed and wanted. It's possible that hereditary hearing loss, through my paternal grandmother's side of the family, had been added on to the nerve damage done by the mumps.

If, speaking metaphorically again, using a behind-the-ear hearing aid had, for me, been like getting around on a motorbike, I was now, thanks to the cochlear implant, about to be strapped into a jet plane! I knew, though, that I wouldn't be taking off all at once in one enormous roar. I'd be introduced to different features of this mode of transportation bit by bit over many months as the volume and the quality of the sounds would be adjusted in what are called "mappings."

But what was it going to be like? I'd read a couple of accounts by users who'd gotten their implants a few years after becoming deaf, and what they said sounded, to me, too good to be true. Within a matter of weeks these people were able to chat again on the phone, go to concerts, participate in bridge games, and talk with their spouses in the dark. Everything was rosy for them. I couldn't imagine sixty years of deafness evaporating into thin air in a couple of weeks. On the other hand, I did—playfully—imagine what it would be like if, suddenly, I began hearing again as a six-year-old. As it turned out, what I imagined came close to what actually happened!

It's all come
to this moment:
muddy boots,
wet parka,
cold hands,
the bump
behind my ear
lumpy,
square,
tender,
foreign,
very much there.

Wired to the PC
on Jeanne's desk,
I watch her
while she and Ed watch me.
(Hope stands still

and hushed
in their eyes.)

Jeanne's fingers pause on the keyboard—
she nods—
twenty-two dots within the spiral
on the PC screen
light up bright green

and I'm feeling a pulse,
a throbbing,
a pressure pushing at my brain
followed by another pressure,
another,
and yet another.

Each movement
of Jeanne's fingers on the keyboard
calls forth more pressures:
some hard,
some quick,
all probing.

"What are they?
Are they sounds?"

Jeanne and Ed are grinning.

I DIDN'T GRIN much the first two weeks after activation.
Even now, over three years later, it's hard to describe the

physical sensations I experience—though less frequently than at first—of sound in my brain.

As I see it—or rather as I hear it—sound, any sound, is pressure, and different sounds have varying pressures. The pressure can be anywhere from light to extreme, as well as from gentle to overbearing. Likewise these pressures can be scratchy and pokey. Sometimes they pinch! I'm not talking here about volume, though increased volume can mean increased pressure. If certain sounds make you smile, laugh, jump, cringe, you must know what I'm talking about because you're responding to the pressures. Perhaps the difference between the way you sense sounds and the way I do is that they are all new for me, whereas they are old news to you.

The look of incomprehension on the faces of adults with normal hearing when I try to tell them about this has convinced me we human beings don't instantly, and automatically, know how to use the physical senses when we're born. We *learn* to hear, see, smell, taste, and touch the world. We also *forget* not only how we learned to use these physical senses, we forget what our first encounter with the sensations was like. There's grace in this forgetting, particularly if the experience was painful. I wouldn't be able to use the implant now if, every time I put it on, it affected me in the way described in the next poem. Nor would I be able to use the implant now if my parents hadn't pushed me at age twelve to use The Brick. I might well have lost touch with sound altogether if they hadn't done that, in the same way a limb can atrophy if not used.

> Feel like
> I have a lopsided brain
> being worn thin
> by incessant

sandpapery sounds,
some so high
I have to shut my eyes.

Feel like
I'll never be able to choose
what's coming at me:
background blare,
foreground buzz.
No place to hunker down.
What have I done?

Hearing sound, a sound, any sound, not to mention *many* sounds all at once, was not comfortable. Period. I had gotten myself into this. Period. I couldn't see any way at all out of it. Period.

❧

I WENT OUT to lunch with a friend about ten days after activation and, throughout the meal, was close to tears. I was *still* uncomfortable. *Nothing* I was getting through the implant—and it was at the lowest possible setting—made sense. It was all soup. ("Soup" quickly became my favorite word to describe auditory chaos.) At that moment I badly wanted my old ways of managing and my behind-the-ear hearing aid back.

I didn't tell my friend how I felt, just said I was a little dizzy and left early. On the way home I wept. At this point I had not been teaching for six years, but I kept in touch with several former students, all of whom had implants and knew I'd just had surgery. I emailed one of them. Hannah, who was born deaf, whom I'd seen travel from hearing aids to two implants over the course of eight years, replied within the hour. Within another

Hannah's wedding day, August 18, 2012.

hour two other former students added their encouragement to hers, also by email. Talk about deafness: they sure weren't deaf to my need in that moment!

> The children
> have become my mentors.
>
> Just a little while ago
> I was the one in the lead—
> or so I thought.
> My job
> was to support them.
>
> Today,
> altogether discouraged,
> Hannah catches me
> by the ear lobes
> as I sink down.

"Hey there!"
It's a command.
"Things *will* get better!"
She's been through this,
twice too.

Her certainty
yanks me upright.

People who are experiencing hearing loss later in life have often told me, "I'm too old to learn to speechread, you can't teach an old dog new tricks." Or "I haven't the energy to get used to a hearing aid or go through surgery for a cochlear implant." I sympathize because adjusting to hearing loss *does* require effort. No question about that. But it never crossed my mind that I was too old to get the cochlear implant. All I knew was that I wanted *something*: more sound, an improvement, a change, a better way of connecting with others, a way that made me a bit less dependent on my eyes. Those things motivated me to make the effort. And in this early stage, when the going was tough, there was this wonderful, instantaneous response from these young people to the effort I was making. "Hang in there!" "Keep going!" was what they told me. Their certainty and energy poured into me, would not let me falter. It didn't matter that I had been their teacher and they were younger than me. My ideas about older and younger, more experienced and less experienced, weaker and stronger, were turned upside down. Help really *is* right here, near where we are, when we most need it!

First Mapping

Jeanne's calm
permeates the office,
calls up the calm
of pink geraniums
on sunny window sills
blooming slowly,
graciously,
all winter long.

Hooked up,
a long dark wire
connecting my head to her PC,
twenty-two dots in the spiral
glowing green,
I signal the number of beeps I'm hearing.

The deep ones are easiest,
most familiar,
most comfortable.
"Two."
"Three."
"Two."

The high ones
startle, prick, tease
"Two . . ."

(Ouch!
OUCH!)
". . . or is that three?"

My brain reaches out
recoils,
reaches out again.
I seem to have huge swaths
of ultrasensitive,
naked, eager brain cells
I was never aware of
till now.

As with the optician
one lens of sound
slips over another,
is taken away
reinserted,
removed again.

"One beep?" asks Jeanne.
"Yes!"

Single beeps are harder to get,
I begin to think
I'm imagining them.
Two, three, or four beeps in a row
confirm each other.

"You say this sound is better?"
"Yes."

"And is this better than that?"
"Hmmm . . . "

I'm not sure.

She presses another key.

I'm getting confused.
How can one sound be "better" than another?
Aren't sounds meant to fit together,
round about, into each other?

Sensing I've reached the limit
of the moment
Jeanne unhooks me,
attaches the wire to my processor,
bends over the PC,
and like a magician,
does some quick finger incantations.

Minutes later she gives me the processor.

As the two magnets snap together
I hear
first a crackling
then,
very clearly,
very distinctly,
Jeanne's voice,
and I *know* it's her voice.

"Is that better?"

"YES!"
I nearly fall off my chair.
Everything is SO much better!

Suddenly all the pressures, pulses,
zig-zags,
rips, buzzes,
and cracklings
are coming into focus,
are becoming
definite forms,
things
places,
people—
rather than gray lumpy bumps
on a map.

I N T H E P R O C E S S of getting the implant this was, without
question, the most exciting moment of all for me.

The hearing aid had, for fifty-five years, brought me sounds
in a rather one-dimensional manner. Sound was loud—that was
it. There were few variations. As a teen I could not, for example,
distinguish between the radio and the record player, which my
mother often played at the same time. For me they were a heck
of a lot of noise. Loud noise. But with the hearing aid, I knew
my mother was engaged with sounds coming from the one and
from the other. As I could see she was listening to this loud
activity and responding to it with interest, pleasure, and sometimes laughter, the aid backed up, verified, and complemented
the hearing I was doing with my eyes. With time I learned to

use *everything* I could to get the information I needed. Though I couldn't, with the hearing aid, hear the way people with normal hearing did, without it I felt less aware, less connected.

Then the implant put me *in* sound. When it was activated, I was shaken by the experience of sound suddenly being all around. It wasn't only loud, it was soft and hard, bright and dim, sometimes closer, sometimes further away. Sound had become three-dimensional and extremely physical, as I described earlier in terms of feeling varying pressures. But I couldn't grasp any of it, was quite disoriented, and, at moments, in pain.

During the first mapping—I love how expressive and how accurate the term is—Jeanne, my audiologist, helped me to orient myself in sound. In the poem I compared it to being at the eye doctor and, by repeatedly trying different lenses, finding the right adjustment in order to see better. As I had been hearing through my eyes for years now, suddenly, I found myself trying to see by way of hearing! Trying to "see" what these sounds were, how they moved, where they came from, and more. You'll be hearing a lot about my discoveries in the pages ahead.

People may think one simply switches to vision if one's hearing doesn't work. In short, one sense compensates for the absence of the other. Yes, it is definitely true that vision usually becomes the dominant sense in deafness, but, for me, there's always been more to it than that. Because of the need to use *everything*, meaning all my senses, to get information in order to connect, I have never thought of the working of the senses as separate activities. For example, take the interweaving of sight, scent, and touch when walking through a forest beside a stream. I "hear" movements of wind and water through the visible movements of leaves, branches, foam and eddies, and through temperature, current, and smell. Smell? Yes! In this

Hiking in the White Mountains of New Hampshire.

instance standing water smells different from flowing water. Translate that into "marshy" or "muddy" areas. Through the sense of smell, it's possible to know when one is coming to a quieter, less active, spot. Add the cochlear implant and these experiences are not only rounded out but greatly amplified.

In a similar vein I want to add here that even before I began to make use of a hearing aid, I've always been aware of an auditory dimension to seeing. Perhaps I'm going by way of memory of what I heard as a child. I don't know about this because I could never reconcile what I heard through the hearing aid with what I remembered of sound. Anyway, this auditory dimension to seeing ranges from simple images and sounds—like seeing breaking waves and hearing sounds similar to *heave, slop, slosh,* and *splash*—to more complex images. I've tried over the years

to express this in poetry. Here is an example of what I mean in
three poems about color.

GREEN

No other color
has so many tones.
Hear the thrilling
young greens in the spring,
then the song deepens
as the days grow longer:
buds, leaves, grasses,
vines, shrubs, trees.
On and on goes the round,
till emerald darkens
and becomes amber,
the song fades out
first here, then there—

Yet the mosses hum on,
the evergreens also
will not let the tune stop.
For what is green
in all her notes
if not the song of hope?

YELLOW

Yellow warms us, it rejoices,
it moves out and out.
It reaches, stretches, slips

into blue and brings green.
It dares red to brighten into orange,
it dares us to look it full in the face:
can we . . . with all our shadows?
It speaks of the first light,
and the last light: dawn and dusk.
And when we think there is no light
It is in the wink of a star.

RED

"Look at me!" says red
as it shines on an apple,
unfolds in a rose,
spurts from a wound.
Red is the badge of anger
and the mask of shame.
It is the first flush of love,
The steady beat of a heart,
then the burning horizon
at the end of the day.

M Y FIRST MAPPING jolted me awake to the possibility
that sounds can also have colors—and textures, sizes,
and shapes! It took me a while to realize this, to begin to separate out these noises and find the words to describe them.

There are four settings on the processor that Jeanne adjusts
whenever I have a mapping. Although Jeanne has explained the
features of each setting to me, I'll admit I have not explored the
differences between them in a thoughtful and scientific way. I'm

not very good when it comes to understanding and tinkering with technology. Each of these four settings can be set lower or higher, and I know that level four brings me more sounds than the three lower levels, so I generally don't go near it when in a noisy, busy environment.

During the first year after surgery I continued to have mappings every three months, as Jeanne tuned me in slowly to more and more sounds of different levels and volumes at each of the settings. She knew better than I what adjustments would be best because of her knowledge of the nature of sound and how much I could tolerate. Once I asked if she would put all the settings a bit higher, and she paused before saying, "It's a lot quieter in here in my office than outside." I thought I was up to the challenge, so she put them at a slightly higher setting, and on the way home I had to pull the processor off and toss it onto the passenger seat because of the ghastly roar of trucks all around. Even in the relative quiet of our house I kept the processor at level one, the very lowest setting, for two weeks. When I went to her next, I admitted she'd been right, and as I was by then able to digest levels one and two and was happy with them, she only tweaked things a bit.

Apart from a yearly checkup, I can ask her for a mapping anytime, whenever I feel the need to get a better grasp of what I'm hearing with the cochlear implant. It is wonderful to have someone to work with in this way. I could not, during my first year with the cochlear implant, have found my way into sound without her assistance.

Baby Steps: Early Discoveries and Observations

In the beginning the most striking, startling, part of using the implant came during the first few seconds, when the inner and outer magnets snapped together connecting my brain with the outer world of sound. Though I'm much less aware of this now, I still occasionally hear this wild noise at the moment the connection occurs. Early on I tried to describe it in verse:

> If I could see
> the sharp splintery,
> crickly-crackly
> sounds that prick my brain
> in the moment
> when the magnets snap together,
> what would they look like?
> Volcanic sparks shooting upward?
> Fire jumping from sprig to sprig?
> Lightning webbing through the heavens?

For about ten days, when I first turned the processor on, I'd glance around the room to see where these crickly-crackly sounds were coming from. I thought maybe they were from the heating system in our house or even my computer. Then I realized they weren't coming to me from outside, they were occurring *within* me. They were, so to speak, start-up sounds.

I know this because I don't hear these sounds if the processor is off when I put it on my head. What I hear in this moment does not have to do with the magnets themselves but with the electric impulses from the processor rushing into my cochlea, from electrode to electrode, on up the auditory nerve and into my brain.

The very first time I heard these sounds—when the implant was activated—I was rattled. It was my idea of what a raging fire must sound like. Then, seconds later, other quite different sounds—sounds from the outer world—began coming in, and I thought, "Whew! Whatever that was—it's gone!"

But then it happened again the next morning, and the next, in fact every time I first put the implant on. I began to think of it as my Michelangelo moment. If you're familiar with his painting of God touching the finger of Adam on the ceiling of the Sistine Chapel, you'll know what I mean. The finger of sound has touched my brain. As I connect with it, the vitality of sound zaps me awake.

❧

A T THE OTHER end of the spectrum, when I turned the implant off, I didn't automatically step back into a silent world. For about six months after the surgery I was often bothered by a condition known as tinnitus, but only after I took the processor off. Tinnitus is usually defined as a roaring or ringing sensation in the ears. It's known to affect people with normal hearing as well as those with hearing loss, whether or not they're wearing a hearing aid or their implant is on. It can be quite debilitating, as it's not only annoying and distracting, it hurts.

Sometimes—
can't escape sound
now that it's found
an inlet,
it goes churning
round-round my head
rolling-roaring
long after
the machine's come off.

Or else
my hyped-up head
can't quit playing tag
with the noises of the day—
slip-slap-pop-thump!
Echoing round-round
my brain
till sleep abruptly
stops the game.

When I signed the medical papers before the operation, I
knew the implant might cause tinnitus. I'd experienced it a few
times in my life, and it was no fun. It was impossible to get
away from, even if I lay down in a dark room and shut my eyes.
The good news for me, though, was that I was still able to fall
asleep, and when I awoke, it was almost always gone.

When I went to Jeanne for my second mapping, I told her
about it and said it was as though some of the sounds that
came to me were "stuck" in my head, like a bunch of Mexican
jumping beans in a box. Jeanne said there was some thought
that the auditory nerve, having been stimulated by the implant,

continues to reach or "grasp" for sounds after the processor is
turned off, causing the tinnitus. In my case it has, thankfully,
stopped. I don't know why, anymore than I know what caused
it, though I do believe stress was a factor—the stress of having
so much sound coming in all at once. As you'll see in the next
four poems, I was on overload.

> Many streams rushing
> to become one
> hurry, eddy, roar,
> gush, tumble, jostle
> in my head,
> till there's no way
> but to close the eyes,
> surrender,
> let the current
> hurtle on ahead.

> Some sounds appear
> in a rush,
> uninvited,
> no time
> to ask,
> "Who are you?"
> "Where did you come from?"
> "What do you mean?"
>
> There's no modesty
> in their coming,
> they don't wait
> on my recognition,

even before I've named them
they're on their way
off . . .
    Clunk!
       Whirr!
          Gone!

One sound
cuts off another—
shrill kettle whistle,
blaring horn,
piercing call—

I feel it
as dislocation,
the moving joint
yanked suddenly
out of its socket,

the attention
caught naked,
wide open,
forced to retreat,
stunned.

All these new sounds,
energies, pressures, powers,
worlds to explore—or—
when the pulse is too great
to retreat from!

How can I retreat
for long
now that I begin to sense
what's been missing?

Can I put it all together?
Am I equal to it?

✺

EARLIER I mentioned imagining—playfully—what it would be like if, suddenly, I began hearing again as a six-year-old. As though picking up my hearing where it had been left off. The fact of the matter is that often, in response to the complexity and glut of incoming sounds, I felt even younger than six years old! Younger than six when it came to coping with sounds, yet my full sixty-seven years when I saw how people everywhere—not just my family and close friends—expected this amazing bit of technology to "cure" deafness. It is always, *always*, touching, this belief in technology, in the power of the human mind and imagination to help the human body. I, too, share it.

Yet, the expectation that the implant does away with deafness continues to be an interesting, and sometimes discouraging, fact. I guess a not-so-helpful aspect to our belief in technology is that we have a need to believe in absolutes. People will ask if I now have 100 percent hearing. Is there is such a thing as 100 percent hearing? Do I really hear what you hear and do you really hear what I hear, sentence by sentence, word for word? Yes, maybe, but, as is evident on so many levels—personal, social, political—you and I may "hear" the exact same words, yet may listen to, interpret, and act on them

in entirely different ways. And later we might disagree on what
we heard to begin with.

Two Months after Surgery

People assume
I'm now like them,
can talk on the phone
(or will soon),
listen to the radio,
participate fluently
in group conversations,
go to concerts
and come out dancing.

They can't see
I'm a baby all over again,
intrigued by this whoosh
and that whap,
rattled by the sandpapery edge
of certain voices,
startled and fatigued
by the sudden snap, screech, squeal,
sheer volume of it all.

Dan, with the bushy beard
greets me with whiskey glee,
benevolence misting his eyes,
except I still can't pull
sentences from the thicket

of gray-black hairs, can't shimmy
down the line of easy gab,
can only watch
while disappointment floods his face,
the pink curves
of his half-hidden lips
looking very much
like the curves
of his eager, cupped ears.

So, slowly, gradually, day by day, I began to find my way.

In my office, on the second floor, I could identify and remember sounds within the house: the vacuum cleaner, the
kettle whistling on the oven top, the oven timer, Ed coming up
the stairs, step by step—which meant he could no longer sneak
up on me and catch me unawares!

Upstairs,
downstairs,
in the other room

you're no longer far away—
footsteps, shaver, sneeze, cough,
can even hear you talking

with the crackly voice
coming through the phone.
Though I only hear the tone

I know I'm not alone,
I know as I have never known
the sounds within a home.

There were all sorts of discoveries to be made outdoors, too, in the deep of winter:

> My toes knew it,
> now my ear hears it:
> ice is often crackly,
> snow can be crunchy,
> frozen earth
> has a low clop.

> A xylophone has emerged
> left and right
> forward and backward
> beneath my feet.
> Weight, will, and walk determine
> how the percussion
> will go.

I think it's the wind . . .

> I.

> Often
> when walking
> someone comes along with me,
> leans close to my head
> makes scraping noises
> as though filing off
> the edge of my ear,
> whispers gibberish,
> gives an eerie laugh,

thumbs through my hair
backward, forward,
backward again,
snorting softly,
hunting for the number
into my brain.

2.

Sometimes
I have to turn to find it,
turn and turn
to listen in,
turn until
I catch the tune,
and we're dancing!

Meanwhile, the sounds I myself made were becoming familiar to me, were no longer a total shock. Imagine suddenly hearing the vigorous rush of your own pee or the rude honk of your own fart!

Around the start of the fifth month I began to tire of the endless questions from others: "What's it like?" "What did you hear this week?" "Are you hearing like before you lost your hearing?" and more. Here are two poems from my journal written at this time.

What do I have to report?

The extraordinary
is becoming ordinary—

shuffling slippers
rub on the stone floor,
tinkle of tableware
has lost its musical clink,
a glass shatters—
I jump—
as sound
fragments into
a hundred pieces.

My own breathing
no longer embarrasses me—
nasal clog, sniffle, snort,
uphill rasp,
deep, dreary sigh.

I guess I
am arriving.

Every day
a new world
flows by
with its onward
push-shove
rip-rustle-ripple
of noises
going, going—

There isn't time—
and increasingly
no need—

> to name them all.
> Either I struggle
> to stay upright,
> head above the waves,
> or dive in.

I wanted to withdraw a bit from the questions, warm and well-meaning as they were. I wanted to ponder my experiences on my own. Put another way, I found the questions tiring rather than stimulating. No matter what form of aid I am using—hearing aid or cochlear implant—fatigue has always, all my life, been a big factor for me. Like other deaf people I simply *have* to get my sleep, deep and regular, or I'm not much fun to be with. Our younger daughter, who spent a semester abroad in Bali, mentioned experiencing the same exhaustion while trying to pick up another language. Likewise the German wife of a cousin of mine said it was years before she was able to relax and enjoy parties in this country. Trying to understand the varying accents and idioms of English wore her out.

As a child there were days when I was so exhausted when I came home from school I'd go straight to bed without supper. Here's another poem written from the point of view of a deaf child on this topic.

> I love going to bed at the end of the day,
> taking off the machinery:
> glasses, aids, batteries, ear molds, tubing . . .
> no FM, no microphone,
> no wire attaching me to them.
>
> When I close the door I'm free,
> free of the need to look, look, look,

watch, watch, watch,
listen, listen, listen.

The outside voices
fade into the distance:
Didyougetit?

Did you get it?

    Did you . . .

        get . . .

           . . . it?

I love the "You can shut down now"
that comes when I turn the lights off,
sink into the warmth, the softness of my bed,
my nest,
my cozy cockpit.
I snuggle down deep,
both arms tight under my tummy
right cheek against the pillow.

Colors fade away
into black-gray-black,
bits of white poke out here and there,
tease my eyes,
warn me
there could be masked men,
smoking, tottering towers,
hungry rats, growling bears.

And I don't care,

I'm on the countdown to sleep,

I'm heading off in my rocket ship

for a distant star,

a star called Come As You Are.

From Baby Steps to Toddler Steps: Explorations in Listening

THE NEXT notable aspect of using the implant became clear to me not suddenly, as when the magnets clicked together, but over time. It had to do with my ability—or my inability—to pay attention. What I have to say may sound elementary, but for me, the discovery was about as significant as learning to stand up.

First I "hear" a sound. If I bring my attention to it, I begin to "listen" to it. When I "listen" to it, I enter into a relationship with the object from which it comes. Listening means meeting, and it means a kind of intimacy, even if only momentary. The relationship can be very quick, very brief. For example, I go from "hearing" a shrill sound downstairs to knowing it's water boiling in the kettle. I know it's the kettle because I've focused my attention on the whistle and have likely gone downstairs to investigate where it's coming from. (Ed is still, three years later, answering the "What's that?" question for me since I can't, physically, get to every place where every sound is coming from.)

If you are a hearing person, you focus your attention, or withdraw it from what you are hearing, thousands of times a day without thinking about it, in the same way you stand up and walk around without thinking about that. You go from "hearing" to "listening" (read that as recognizing or identifying what the sound is) back to "hearing." In forming a "relationship" with the kettle, once can be enough. For me it was enough. But, with other sounds, the human voice in particular, a whole new world was opening up. I've always been sensitive to the vibration of voices, particularly deep-toned voices resounding on my chest when people are talking. When I was a child and my father came into my room to say good night, I couldn't see him in the dark, but I could feel his words and I knew it was him. I could not sense my mother's voice in the same way because it was higher. Sometimes I could also feel the vibrations from strongly expressed emotions, like anger. It is no surprise to me how dogs often draw their ears back when people are shouting, even if the shouting is not directed at them. I believe they're trying to protect themselves from the vibrations.

Now the cochlear implant was taking me to another level of hearing and listening to the human voice. The essence of this discovery was that, quite apart from conveying information through spoken language, the human voice is amazingly expressive. Tone can say as much as, sometimes more than, the words we use. When I brought my attention to bear on what I was hearing—as, for example, when Ed was speaking—there were so many things to listen to!

Here's what I heard one evening as we were having supper:

> Listening
> to the sound of your voice
> I let go of the need
> to find meaning.
>
> Keep talking!
> Let the words roll,
> dip, dive, bob up,

pollywog wonders
wiggling around
in the air
between us.
Wrap me double
in the warmth
of the deep notes
I now know
are you.
Allow me to touch
the texture
of your breathing-in-speaking.
Tickle me
with your laugh.

Equally exciting was another discovery. After a lifetime of watching people's faces and "listening" to their expressions, I found most people *sound* the way they look! I happened upon this realization during a weekly meeting at work. Twelve of us were sitting around an oval table discussing an upcoming conference. It was about three months after surgery, I still tired quickly, and had closed my eyes for a few seconds to take a break.

In those few seconds I heard someone talking. I couldn't get what was being said, but I was pretty sure Deb was speaking. I opened my eyes, peeked, and sure enough, it *was* Deb! Astonished and instantly refreshed, I shut my eyes and listened for another voice. A minute later I concluded only Melissa talked in the pace and tone I was hearing, and yes, it was Melissa! And so on almost around the whole table. There was something deeply reassuring about this discovery. Reassuring not so much

in the sense that I was learning to recognize voices, but in the
sense that we are who we are *all the way through*, in the same
way a rose is a rose is a rose!

> This face
> has that voice.
>
> Now
> after years
>
> of knowing one
> but not the other
>
> there's deep
> contentment
>
> in fitting
> the two together.
>
> As blue and yellow
> unite in green,
>
> salt and pepper
> shape the taste,
>
> left and right
> create the clap,
>
> form *and* tone
> complete your name.

With time I found I could also sometimes recognize the sound of a person's voice without the person having to be present. This happened months later when I took our car to be serviced. As I was waiting in line to discuss possible repairs with the man at the desk, a loud voice suddenly came on in the background. I assumed I was hearing someone on a radio and noticed how others in line with me stopped talking among themselves and began listening. Though I couldn't understand what was being said, I knew I'd heard this voice before.

"*Who* is it?" I kept wondering.

Minutes later, after talking with the serviceman, I rounded the corner into the waiting room, looked up, and there was President Obama giving a speech on TV. I had, from listening to other speeches by him on TV, recognized his tone and measured pace. ("Professorial" was the word Ed used when I asked how he would describe Obama's voice in this circumstance.)

All of this led me to consider the overall "feel" of language when not listening to it specifically for meaning and content. I thought of what I was listening for as texture, color, even weight, because, as you surely know, words can come out sounding heavy as well as light.

To explain this from another angle, it might help for me to say a bit more about the different ways I've learned to listen with my eyes.

I have always felt the need to go beyond mere speechreading when people are speaking. As mentioned earlier, I learned as a child to read faces as well as lips, and I discovered that when the mouth is saying one thing, the eyes may be saying something quite different. A simple example of this is when someone you're close to says, "I'm okay," but you know from the expression in that person's eyes she isn't okay at all. I'm pretty sure hearing people pick up on little things like this all the time, often without realizing it. They may say they have an intuition when they're actually having a very subtle perception. The more aware you become of these little perceptions, the more you see and hear them. It's not that you go around doubting people or second-guessing them, it's that, when you're not getting information through the usual routes, you become more observant.

The need to read the *whole* face, and bodily gestures as well, not just what's coming out of the mouth, is reinforced by the fact that it's extremely hard to speechread every word in a sentence. Many words can't be seen on the lips, particularly if the person mumbles, has a mustache or an accent, or doesn't look directly at you. In addition, there are the absolutely essential words and the less essential words. The absolutely essential words are those that identify the topic of the conversation. This is why, when in a group and a deaf person asks what you just said, it might be more helpful if you identify the topic ("We're talking about dogs") rather than trying to repeat word for word what you said. ("I was talking about when I was a little kid, our family went on a trip to the animal shelter in another state, and we found our first dog.") When you know the topic, it's much easier to hitch a ride onto the rest of what's being said—because you're on the lookout for that topic—while letting the less essential words, like adverbs and prepositions and even some adjectives, drop by the roadside. (The deaf are great at getting right to the point of what's being said! In some situations I have very little patience or energy for chitchat. I think this could be called a survival mechanism, as our ability to pay attention is not without limits.)

Hearing often "catches" what's invisible to the eyes. If the conversation is about dogs, the word "dog" will likely keep coming up. Likewise, the names of different breeds of dogs may come up, or dog behavior, or dog paraphernalia—and you'll be on the alert for all of that. When I said yes to getting the implant, I knew I wanted and needed more basic information in everyday conversations. I knew I was slowing down a bit, and it seemed to me that conversations, particularly among young people, were speeding up. Add to that a faltering digital hearing aid and more hearing loss: there were just too many glaring gaps in what I was hearing.

During my first year with the implant, I was, while hearing more sounds, applying the same approach to hearing with one ear that I had applied to speechreading with my eyes. I was doing this out of habit. As speechreading means more than reading words on the lips, hearing means more than hearing words as they are spoken. As stated a few pages back, I was going beyond just listening for meaning in words. To speak metaphorically, I wasn't just trying to identify each flower in the garden, I was noticing color combinations, shapes created by many flowers, and more. Put yet another way, I believe I now hear *many* sounds within every sentence. Even single words may be composed of more than one sound. In everyday conversation the exchange of thought is so central and often so rapid there isn't time to think about these nuances. Whether these nuances are due to changes in volume and stress, or shifts from vowels to consonants, I don't know. The poems I wrote about this may better express these observations than prose.

New roundness,
color,
structure,
and spacing

of the spoken word
        amazes,
                delights,
                        distracts—

whole sentences
are gardens
        planned,
                random,
        large,
                small,
        groomed,
                overgrown,

places I hadn't realized existed
in simple exchanges
till lit up
by sound.

What does it mean
when there's
this tissue-papery rustle
around your words?

Am I hearing
your stuffed up nose
or is this wrapping
in my head?

Single words
are wrapped
in their own
special wrapping.

"Hi."
"Well . . ."
"Damn!"
"Bye-bye—"

Crisp.
Rumpled.
Muffled.
Torn.

Whole sentences
become rustling tissue,
crackly cellophane,
gritty sandpaper.

Sometimes the brain
gives up
before it can
open and find the meaning
in this avalanche
of packages.

My Own Voice

AND THEN I heard my own voice!

Before describing this meeting, I want to give you some background and share with you the third lesson deafness taught me when I was a child.

When I wore a hearing aid, both as a child and as an adult, I couldn't really hear myself. The aid gave me some sense as to whether I was speaking in a loud or soft voice, but not always. Many were the times my parents, my brother, and later, Ed and our daughters, would signal to me, "People can't hear you. . . speak up!" or "Shhh. . . you're shouting!" (Actually it still happens now and then. Either old habits die hard, or I'm louder than I realize!)

Making oneself understood through speech can be as hard for the deaf person as hearing and understanding what others are saying. It's particularly hard for the child who is born deaf. A hearing child will likely have a vocabulary of about three thousand words by the age of four. A child of the same age who was born deaf and has no immediate access to hearing aids, an implant, or American Sign Language, may know only about three hundred words! (Babies can now get implants when they're only twelve months old. In the past hearing aids were often introduced when the child was quite a bit older, depending, of course, on the type of loss and when it was diagnosed.) I was *very* lucky to have soaked up many words and much grammar before the age of six. In short, I knew what spoken language was all about, and how it went. But, without any hearing aid, and I didn't get one for another six years, I was in a danger zone.

My parents' major concern was that I might stop talking. Then, unable to participate in ordinary everyday conversation where one monitors and corrects oneself by way of hearing, my speech would disintegrate. They arranged for hours of speech therapy. Told to repeat words, sentences, and meaningless jingles over and over, the weekly appointments and follow-up practice sessions at home often had me in tears. The therapist might, for example, suddenly interrupt me with "That's right!" and I'd have no idea how what I'd just uttered differed from what I'd said two minutes earlier. Once my mother, in an attempt to *show* me how I sounded, grabbed a bunch of grapes, stuffed them in her mouth and mumbled something. I was, of course, unable to read her lips. Though that might seem now like a harsh way to make a point, I got it and slowed down.

At the same time I discovered how bluffing my way through conversations—pretending I understood what was being said rather than adding to the conversation by admitting I didn't— was a lot less jarring and less tiring than having to ask people to repeat what they'd said or having to repeat what I'd said. I figured if I couldn't get the information at the moment, like in the middle of a class, I could get it later. I didn't want to be a drag or a distraction on regular everyday conversations among my hearing peers or in family gatherings.

There are several degrees of bluffing. At one end of the spectrum is timid, sleepy fakery. For example, a person may do what he sees everyone else doing without really being aware of the speech, and thoughts, accompanying the actions. It doesn't matter to him if he misses the content, he just goes along with it all. At the other end of the spectrum, a person may see when someone is going to try to engage him and will deliberately look away or move elsewhere to avoid making contact. The more one does this, the more one gets into the habit of retreating. This is common among deaf and hard of hearing people of all ages. My mother understood this danger very clearly and pushed hard against it. I'll be returning to the topic of bluffing later—but for now I want to share what I had to learn when I was twelve years old.

❧

The Third Lesson

I not only got my first hearing aid when I was twelve, I also got braces, glasses, and something else. Whatever the season, whatever the weather, I wore long, shapeless sweaters in an effort to hide not only The Brick, but to hide the twin peaks emerging on either side of it!

I also left public school, where I wasn't doing very well, and entered a local private school for girls, repeating the seventh grade. Much later I learned the school made an agreement with my parents to give me a try for one year. If I measured up, I'd be allowed to continue. The second year also was conditional. By the third year I'd earned my place. My parents were eager to keep me in mainstream schools. They looked at one school for the deaf early on, and the story goes, were so bothered by the "deaf accents" of the children they feared I might *become* deaf if I went there!

I know now my parents' choices were absolutely right for me every step of the way, but at age twelve I was in the midst of an inner tsunami. Not only was I entering adolescence, the schoolwork was harder than anything I'd ever done and the classes were much smaller (meaning I couldn't get away with bluffing). Most troubling of all, I wasn't sure *who* I was.

Let me add there were none of the classroom aids for the deaf that are available today: note takers, interpreters, oral translit-erators, closed captioning, FM systems, email, texting phones, the Internet, and so on. Deafness wasn't talked about, either at home or at school. Why not? Though my mother in particular was extremely honest with me whenever she thought I could do better—and she genuinely wanted this for my own good—I believe my parents thought talking about deafness was com-plaining. And one did not complain, one pushed on, did one's best, and that was that. I can recall occasions when my father told me I would be able to hear and talk on the telephone again as I had done when six years old if I just tried harder. And, in this department, I couldn't do it, I just couldn't measure up to what he thought I could do.

I don't think my parents wanted to shame or punish me, they simply did not know what it was like for me. My father had great faith in science, medicine, hearing aids, and the power of the human mind to figure things out and correct or improve them. In addition, my parents did not want me to feel sorry for myself. When I was moody, they'd say, "Snap out of it!" They looked for what I *could* do and dared me to do what I could in those areas. My mother signed me up for ballet, so I'd be con-scious of how I moved and wouldn't have a loud, heavy walk. I loved dance and dreamt of being a sugarplum fairy in *The Nutcracker*. Tennis was also pretty important in our family, and we played together frequently. Maybe my parents preferred the idea of my writing plays or novels instead of poetry, maybe my mother thought pottery, which I took to with great enthusiasm

Graduation from Bennington College.

when in college, was mere craft beside the art of painting, but whenever I found something I liked to do, I did it for myself, not to please them. They honored that, wanted copies of my published work, kept some of my ceramics, and were proud of my independence.

I have heard quite a few stories like my own from others my age or older, who were born deaf, or who became deaf when they were quite young and were mainstreamed. Deafness and how it affected us emotionally were not discussed. Today we call this denial. Back then, talking about our feelings meant we were indulging in them. The critical view that prevailed was, I guess, considered the necessary road to improvement, and my parents were doing what most people did then. It is clear, abundantly clear, when I talk today with parents of young deaf children that technology and our understanding of deafness are not the only things that have evolved, because these parents *want* to know what the deaf experience is like. Compassion and empathy have also evolved. Consider how we accept as normal and necessary the reservation of parking spaces for the disabled. Or the prevalence of ASL interpreters at public events. There's always more that waits to be discovered when it comes to understanding and helping one another.

To return to me as a twelve-year-old.

The closest I came to talking about what it was like to be deaf was with my speech therapist, who tried to make sounds visible. She would use Kleenex tissues, feathers, and candle flame. If the tissue went too high, or the feather bent, or the flame flickered wildly when I spoke, the sounds I was making were too strong. She also called on my sense of touch, placing my fingers on her lips, cheeks, or throat, to enable me to "hear" the sounds that aren't visible on the lips. While my parents approached good speech as a matter of will power, done primarily through drilling and daily practice, the therapist emphasized feeling. Not emotional feeling about what I was doing, but my felt-sense of the mechanics of the act of speaking. I could *feel* the difference when I was trying to speak clearly, distinctly, word by word, and when I was jumbling things up (which happens when I'm tired). This felt sense of how I am forming words as I say them is still strong today, and the result is a form of over-enunciation. I'm often embarrassed when looking at photos or videos of myself talking because the way I talk looks so laborious! How puckered up my mouth is! How much I use my eyebrows and my hands! Sometimes I look as though I'm making up my own sign language. (I do know some American Sign Language, find it beautiful and very expressive, but am not fluent in it.)

Later, a few years after the occasion I want to share with you, there was someone at the school I attended whom I might have talked with about deafness, but right then, mainstream schooling was, for me, a sink-or-swim situation. I did not realize it at the time, but I can see that now. I always had to sit up front, near the teacher who usually walked around the classroom or turned her back to me while writing on the board, making speechreading impossible. To compensate, I learned to read ahead of the class and to read more than was required. Luckily I love to read.

Yes, what I'm describing may sound difficult. And, yes, again, there's no question education of the deaf today is a completely different story, thank goodness, but I believe I was lucky not only because I had six years of hearing under my belt but also because I lost my hearing when I did. Had I been older, like twelve and on the cusp of adolescence, my focus would, very likely, have been on the social scene and what I was missing. Though I *was* aware in elementary school of other kids, I was not uncomfortable in the solitude imposed on me by deafness. One reason for this is that during the time I had no hearing aid, I experienced an inner presence that spoke to me calmly, sensibly, and lovingly whenever I was upset, confused, or lonely. You may remember how I prayed to God right after I lost my hearing. I continued, in my own fashion, to pray, and still do. I did not see anyone but never doubted what I heard, and best of all, I could hear this inner voice perfectly without any effort. I might hear, "You're okay," and I believed it and went right on.

Or, "Go help your mother" and would do just that. I always assumed—and I believe the same today—*everyone* whether they have normal hearing or not can connect with this guiding presence. This was independent of participation in any church. I discovered I was not alone.

In the two lessons I shared earlier I realized I was "fine." I was not dumb (meaning stupid), I was not sick or in need (like the leper). But now, as I entered a new school, the outer world was not only pressuring me, it was calling to me, drowning out the inner voice. I was no longer sure I was "fine." I could see how my classmates connected with one another while on the go, and I was excluded from all that.

On this particular occasion my brother was away, and I was having supper with my parents. My father was talking, I was nodding, my mother said something to me, and the next minute she was asking me, very directly and pointedly, what she'd said. I didn't have a clue, but nodded again anyway.

Then her hand came down with a big BANG on the table top making me jump.

"Stop nodding!"

I stared at her.

"Stop pretending!"

I was unable to say anything.

I came *very* close—in the few minutes during which she waited for my response—to throwing my dinner plate across the room!

Instead I yelled back, "I'm sick of this! Why did it happen to me? Why didn't it happen to Judy? (She was the girl next door who wouldn't have anything to do with me.) Why is everyone after me all the time?"

And so on.

I wasn't yelling specifically at my parents. I was yelling at everyone and everything, at what I missed, and was continually missing, the whole exhausting muddle and frustration of being deaf in a hearing world.

I remember clearly the shock on my parents' faces.

Then I ran upstairs to my room, slammed the door, and wept. No one came to tell me I'd be okay because things were *not* okay, and my parents weren't going to yield an inch on my mother's insistence that I stop bluffing.

The anger and frustration that were building up in me had come to a head and burst. The overall effect of this head-on collision with my mother was, for me, relief. And soreness. Soreness because seeing the truth of the matter *can* hurt. Something, in fact, quite a few things, would have to change. How? I didn't know, but I felt better, a lot better, more truly *in* myself in some way.

Let me stress once again that I couldn't articulate what I was going through. But I believe I met deafness—face to face—in this moment. On some inner level I'd acknowledged the limitations that came with it and took on the task of working *with*, rather than against, these limitations. When one works *with* the limitations, one can begin to know deafness as opportunity rather than disability. As Alexander Graham Bell put it so eloquently:

> *When one door closes, another opens; but we often look so long and so regretfully upon the closed door that we do not see the one which has opened for us.*

Before this experience the inner voice had helped me to integrate what the world was telling me or asking of me. When kids were mean, for example, I understood through what I heard inwardly that maybe they didn't know how to be with me or were scared. I could remember how my family reacted to the leper. Now with sounds pouring in through The Brick, school and home pressuring me to be more this and more that, and hormones beginning to heat up, I needed to find my own voice and the ability to speak for myself, beginning with "I didn't get that, please tell me again."

Shortly after this major meltdown, I began keeping the journal into which I poured thoughts and feelings on just about everything. I began writing stories too and several years later became involved in the school newspaper and literary magazine, earning the position of editor. Maybe I couldn't "hear" others, or myself, through my ears, but when I read and when I wrote, I could hear everyone perfectly, could say anything I wanted, didn't have to repeat myself constantly, could travel back and forth in time, could even talk with animals or angels! Writing gave me wings!

In my work with deaf children I've always believed it's *absolutely essential* that the child with hearing loss learn to speak for herself in whatever language is right for her, whether it's spoken English or ASL. The seed of my interest in helping deaf children become self-advocates was sown when I was twelve years old. It would take root as I explored different forms of self-expression in writing and gradually found the courage to draw attention to my presence and what I needed in order to be a contributing member of the different hearing environments I was part of.

Well-meaning parents need to understand this too, or they, in their eagerness to step in and speak for their child at every turn, can actually become a hindrance. I remember how, at the sign-in for a workshop I was giving for deaf teens, both the hearing mother and the older hearing sister of a deaf boy of

Enjoying some one-on-one time at a teen conference.

fourteen answered my questions to him. Parents and siblings were *not* invited to attend this workshop, and I was eager to see how he would manage by himself. Getting him to communicate on his own—to tell the other attendees where he went to school, what it was like being the only deaf kid in that school, how he managed in classes, and what his interests were—was one of the toughest jobs I've ever done. But at the end of the day, he was grinning and excitedly exchanging email addresses with his new friends, kids like him from other mainstream schools, while his mother and sister waited for him just outside the door. Till then he hadn't realized he had a story to tell, the story of who he was and where he came from. Nor did he realize that a new chapter, a chapter focused on his interests and what he knew he was good at, was right then starting to take shape. Being able to talk about baseball as he did that day gave him the impetus to try out for the school baseball team.

Talk about realizations and my own voice: what I did not realize for over fifty years was that when I work at my desk or at the keyboard, I very often *say* the words aloud while writing or typing. The words not only form in my head, they form on my lips. It's as though my tongue and lips need to *feel* the form and *taste* the taste of each word before I can use it. Words really can feel smooth or rough, can taste bitter or sweet! Along a similar line, if I don't know how to pronounce a word, I won't use it. If I encounter it when reading, I'll jump over it. It remains distant, foreign, a stranger, until somebody can write it out phonetically for me to learn to pronounce.

When I got the implant, I discovered this need to articulate words out loud as I'm writing them:

> Before—
> I couldn't hear myself,
> saw when others
> couldn't understand me,
> even wondered at times, "Is my voice real?"
>
> Now—
> I know I can be loud!
> In fact was spooked
> by someone speaking
> when I was writing
> and——it was me!

My family laughed hard when I told them how weird it was to discover that I was the other person in the room. They had often heard me sounding out my sentences in my writing room. They are as familiar with my typing voice as they are with my conversational voice and all the other odd bodily noises I make. When I realized this, I felt as though I'd been walking around naked for most of my life and hadn't been aware of it till then!

And how did my own voice sound to me, *really*?

Loud.

Close.

Very close!

More about Bluffing

THREE YEARS AFTER my meltdown at age twelve described in the last chapter, a new headmistress was hired at my school. Miss McBee was a tall, thin spinster with short straight brown hair, piercing black eyes, dark-rimmed glasses, *and* a modern-day behind-the-ear hearing aid! I had never seen a hearing aid of this sort. In fact, I didn't know for some time what it was until a classmate told me. This was another person I might have discussed deafness with if the tenor of the time had been different.

About two months after she arrived, Miss McBee began looking for me during the morning assembly. She, and others also, made daily announcements, and she wanted to be sure I was getting them. From where she was standing, high up on the stage, she would seek me out in whatever row I happened to be sitting and would move her lips silently asking, "Are you following?"

The first time it happened I was terrified. It was as though a spotlight had been switched on and directed right at me. Rather than responding to her question, I sank down in my seat trying to get out of her line of vision. What was going on? What had I done?

The next day it happened again. This time I knew she really *was* talking to me. I also realized no one, as far as I could see, was aware that she had spoken to me. It was quite thrilling. Here I was in the midst of some two hundred hearing girls who were deaf and blind to the fact that a conversation—albeit a short and simple one—was taking place.

This happened daily. If I passed Miss McBee in the hallway, she'd give a curt or preoccupied nod, such as she gave to any other student. But during announcement time her attention was all mine. You can be sure I was trying to follow those announcements!

One morning during assembly Miss McBee told the student body quite emphatically we were *not* to leave our pocketbooks or other valuables in our open cubbies. (There were no lockers with locks at this school.) We were either to leave them at home or carry them with us everywhere. There had been a rash of small thefts, and she was determined to get to the bottom of the matter.

A couple of days later I came in late after my speech therapy session at the local hospital. I'd forgotten *not* to bring my pocketbook and didn't want to take it to science so shoved it into the back of my cubby, stuffed my scarf, mittens, and coat over it, and dashed off to class.

When I returned to the cubby during recess, the pocketbook was gone!

Indignant, I marched upstairs to Miss McBee's office. She was free, and the secretary ushered me in.

The headmistress was writing at her desk. It was the first time I'd spoken alone with her.

I told her my pocketbook had disappeared.

"Well . . . ," Her dark eyes bored into me. "That's unfortunate."

"I had five dollars in my wallet . . ."

"Did you hear my announcement the other day?"

I nodded. The fact that I'd heard her and hadn't done what she asked seemed, right then, pretty stupid. Who was this thief in our midst? What other valuables had that person taken? Somehow I'd gotten the idea—maybe because of my deafness—I was immune to what was going on.

"Well. . . ." She regarded me for one long moment. "If anything like this happens again, you'll have to accept it as your own fault."

Then she reached down, pulled my pocketbook out from beneath her desk, and handed it to me.

I was stunned.

Nothing more was said.

The next morning during announcements she smiled when she looked my way. To this day I am very sorry we never really talked because Alice McBee was one smart and tender educator. I knew she was looking out for me, and that made me try harder. Though her hearing loss was not as severe as mine, I felt recognized and understood as a deaf person, in a way I had never felt understood before. It was a totally new feeling.

Understanding the speech of others is one thing. Being understood by others is something else. Such understanding makes one feel not just comfortable, but safe. I now know people, mostly educators of the deaf, but there are among them family members such as Ed and our daughters, who know me so well they know what I'm trying to say even when my speech isn't at its best. They know, too, the habits and quirks that accompany deafness. Though this is deeply reassuring for me, I don't know if it's always good. I suspect my speech can become sloppy if I assume others will always get what I'm saying. The cochlear implant brought this possibility home to me early on.

Four to six months after I got the implant, several people told me my voice had changed. When I asked how it had changed, they said it was more varied, more pleasing.

Even I, when I wore a behind-the-ear hearing aid, could hear how there's such a thing as a "Deaf accent." It lacks melody, inflection, variation. It can be shrill, hard, monotonous. I hoped back then that I didn't sound like that, yet had been aware all my life when people found my voice odd. Their faces expressed everything from puzzlement to outright disgust. Sometimes people thought I had a foreign accent and asked where I was from. Sweden? Finland? Russia? It was tempting to name whatever distant country came to mind!

Other times, closer to home, I could see it took a while for my aging parents, for example, to readjust to my speech when they hadn't seen me for a month or more. I referred to this as "getting back onto Claire's channel," but I'll admit I sometimes found it hard to turn it into a joke. It's not fun when people, especially people I am close to, clearly prefer speaking to Ed than to me. My mother was always pretty up front with me when she found my speech hard to follow. Others evidently were not, as I discovered after getting the implant.

It's strange,
unsettling,
altogether rattling
being told,
"Your speech is *so* much better!"

Lee beamed as she said that.
I know she's happy for me
(and for herself)
but what—really—
does she mean?

If she's been pretending all this time—
didn't we first meet in 1967?—
to understand me
and I've—sometimes—
been pretending to understand her,
like when she talks while looking the other way
and I can't see her face . . .

How many years of pretending is this?
How many others feel this way?

The questions make me want to weep.

Why did these questions make me want to weep?

Lee's roundabout admission that she had found it difficult
to understand my speech during all the years I'd known her
made me feel momentarily as though the bottom had dropped
out beneath me. I had been trying and trying to understand
others, and I had been trying and trying to be honest when I
couldn't understand them, and, I guess, I had expected people
with hearing would do the same with me. But it was clear some
hadn't, and that hurt. It was as though numerous conversations
I thought I'd had over the years had suddenly turned out to be
nonexistent, or barely existent. The cochlear implant had not
only brought new connections in every direction, the light it
brought in the form of new connections also revealed shadows
I had not known were there from before I got it. How many
people, really, had, or have, difficulty understanding me? That
was the question.

It brought up a slew of other questions too. Should one tell
another person outright they are hard to listen to or to understand? Is bluffing sometimes kinder? Or is it a cop-out? I've

always said I want people to be direct with me: if we're having difficulty communicating then, let's figure out how we *can* communicate. On the other hand, there are times when the effort of making communication possible seems altogether too exhausting. I know that feeling. It must have been that way for Lee. Though what she said hurt at first, I also knew she didn't mean to hurt me, that she was speaking out of gladness for me. And so we "met" each other in a new way that day.

Is it possible this also happens among people with perfectly normal hearing? For instance, we may understand our neighbor's speech okay, but we may not understand that neighbor's way of thinking. And we might not want to bother to understand, so we bluff. I've done that because I didn't feel up to making the effort. Maybe other things were on my mind, or I was in a hurry somewhere, or I knew to begin with I wasn't going to agree. So why bother?

Communication—true communication—ear to ear, eye to eye, mind to mind, heart to heart: what goes into it, how does it come about? I'm still learning.

This seems a fitting place to put the fourth, and final, lesson from deafness I have to share with you from when I was young.

The Fourth Lesson

Concerned that I might become a recluse, my mother sometimes signed me up to participate in events I had little interest in signing up for myself. Thus it happened that I found myself on a bus one Friday afternoon along with a dozen other girls going to Vermont on a ski weekend.

I was fourteen and was finally beginning to find my way in my new school. (This was about half a year before Miss McBee became headmistress.) I'd discovered I was somewhat athletic, I was on several teams, and one of my stories had just appeared in the literary magazine. Yes, I loved snow, but I had never been on skis before in my life. In addition, I understood from my mother that the teacher in charge of the event had asked the other girls who would be willing to volunteer to share a room with me. The girl who'd volunteered, whose nickname was Bobbie, was two years older than me, and was someone I greatly admired.

It's my observation most teens don't want to get too close to those they admire. They want to do their admiring from a safe distance where their zits, braces, and other foibles are—they hope—well out of sight. Though it was a cold February, I was in a sweat all the way to Vermont! I was going to have to undress and dress in the same space as Bobbie. She was going to see The Brick up close. How were we going to make small talk? How quickly would she discover I couldn't chat in the dark? Most bothersome of all was the possibility she had volunteered to share a room with me because she felt sorry for me.

Speechreading at dinner in the ski lodge that night, as the conversation bounced all over like ping-pong balls, was just about impossible. I decided (1) I was going to be in bed and out of sight early, and (2) my eyes would be closed tight, whether or not I was asleep, when Bobbie went to bed. I was in classic retreat mode! Classic bluffing mode too!

The next morning I was up, dressed, and downstairs before anybody was awake. After breakfast—Bobbie was at the other end of the table—rather than admitting I didn't know how to ski, I followed the others into the rental department at the ski resort, then up the lift to an intermediate trail. It was icy and I realized pretty quickly I'd be lucky if I got down in one piece.

Pretending I needed to adjust some straps, I nonchalantly told the others to go on. The minute they were out of sight, I removed the skis and made my way down, mostly on my rear end! When I finally reached the base camp, I discovered everybody had finished lunch and was heading back to the lift. I stayed on level ground.

That evening, after another dinner with conversational ping-pong balls flying all over, someone suggested playing charades. That would have been about as easy for me as slipping and sliding down the intermediate trail, so I headed for the bedroom. By then Bobbie had given up trying to communicate with me. Who could blame her?

I could not, and did not, want to sleep. All I wanted was to get away from the mess I was in. Walking had always helped when I didn't know what to do, so I dressed again, put on my boots, jacket, and mittens, and slipped out the back door of the lodge.

I walked and walked and walked on the snowy road with no idea as to where I was or what direction I was headed in, and gradually the sheer beauty of that clear winter night dawned on me. There were hundreds of bright, blooming stars overhead. How they sparkled and winked! I'd never seen a sky like this before. As I looked up, my fears, disappointments, and frustrations ebbed away, and the largeness and beauty of the universe flowed in. I don't know how long I stood silently on that snowy road in Vermont basking in starlight.

When I headed back to the lodge, I knew, as I had known when I was six years old, I was not alone. As a child I had discovered that when I heard the voice within. Now I was hearing it from without, not through words as we know them, but through the beauty of the heavens. What I felt was the reality of a divine order. The sun would rise and set; night would flow into day and day back into starry night, even if I slipped and slid around and made a fool of myself. My personal mishaps seemed pretty small beside the majesty of that moment. And now, looking back, they seem pretty comical. I could not, and still cannot, explain where the confidence came from that filled me then. I knew, without knowing how I knew it, that I'd have to take many steps toward the world if I wanted to connect and communicate with others and be part of it. If people didn't come to meet me, I'd have to go to meet them. And the bluffing would have to stop, because saying I did not know how to do something, or did not understand what was going on, might actually be easier than pretending. I've never been much of an actress. Descending that icy trail had been more than scary, it had been terrifying!

I am closing this chapter on bluffing with this story because even now, as old friends continue to comment on my "improved" speech, I realize I can't ask them, "Did you always have difficulty understanding me?" Because it doesn't seem fair to raise the question and make them uncomfortable. Maybe they didn't understand a little—or even a lot—of what I said, but they have stood by me as friends for as long as we've known each other. That is a great kindness. Perhaps we can be stars for each other even if we don't understand one another instantly, or as well, or as deeply as we'd like.

Children

As I said in my introduction, it was children—deaf children—who showed me how the cochlear implant can change the deaf experience. It took me awhile, though, to recognize the magnitude of this change the cochlear implant has brought about. It took me a while because (1) I was so deeply embedded in my own experience of deafness and my dependence on speechreading and face reading I could not imagine it being any other way, and (2) I'll admit there has always been something in me that resists the advance of technology. When word processing first came on the scene and our daughters urged me to try a computer, I told them I had my own method when it came to writing books and, thank you, I was perfectly happy with that. Right now, as I use the computer to write this book, I wonder how in the world I managed to churn manuscripts out on a typewriter, even if it was an electric typewriter.

When I got the implant, I had been a teacher of elementary and middle school children in writing, art, and crafts for twenty-six years. (I also was a kindergarten teacher at the start of my teaching career.) I knew when the children did not understand me—it was easy to see because so much of what I did with them was right there in front of us: drawing, cutting, clay work, weaving, beading, knitting, sewing. The work defined, to a large degree, the nature of our communications. Likewise, in writing, I read what the children wrote and responded in writing. I also knew when there was a discipline problem:

Some of my writing.

those, also, were easy to see and to correct, often with a single glance.

Deep down I also knew I missed a fair amount of what went on in class, mostly when I was with hearing children. (Ed is also an educator. Many of the part-time classes I taught were offered in the schools where he worked.) It was the "unscripted" part of each class when kids talked, joked, and shared stories among themselves that went right by me. Only when I seriously began to consider getting the cochlear implant did I admit to myself how much I had wished for years and years to be able to listen in on these exchanges. For I could *see* how delightful many of them were, could speechread snatches of them now and then, but seldom got the all of anything. I was the outsider, the observer, rarely a participant. I consoled myself with the knowledge that I was the teacher, and the teacher, well, the teacher taught, she didn't fool around with the kids.

First class I taught. Kindergarten 1971–1972, Long Island.

I was not able to work with deaf children as much as I would have liked because there were years when we did not live that close to a school or program for the deaf. Then we moved to western Massachusetts and I discovered Clarke Schools for Hearing and Speech (formerly Clarke School for the Deaf, the first permanent oral school for the deaf founded in 1867). I felt as though I had come home!

Here were deaf children with hearing parents who were acting out of the same deep wish that had shaped the decisions my parents made: they wanted to be able to talk orally with their children and they wanted their children to find their place in the hearing world. Here were children whose facial expressions, thoughts, perceptions, and jokes I could understand at a glance and relate to. And I met not only children enrolled in the Clarke school, but deaf children in regular schools who benefited from Clarke Mainstream Services. I quickly realized Clarke Mainstream Services was the department I wanted most to work in, and I'll never forget an occasion when I was observing a deaf girl in a mainstream class.

It was a fifth-grade class—the girl was was a year older than her classmates, new to the class, and quite a bit taller, and had not yet found a friend or two. She wore one hearing aid. Her teacher later told me privately of her ongoing battle to get her student to wear the hearing aid. Almost daily she "forgot" it at home. I was immediately reminded of the way I had tried as a kid to wiggle out of wearing The Brick.

WHAT THE DEAF GIRL'S EYES SAID

I'm stuck
over here
on the shore
trying not to be
too fishy,
smelly,
weird,
flip-flopping,
fin in the mud,
gills gasping
at the hard air,
eyes glued to the sparkling,
the ever on-going
flow of words,
grins,
laughter,
a mere
splash away,
yet
oh
so
far off.

Teaching on Long Island in the 1970s.

That twelve-year-old girl looked *so* alone! I wept as I drove home that day. Then there were the stories the itinerant teachers shared at Mainstream meetings about other children who were obviously struggling. Only after about a year and a half of observing and listening to stories about these children did it dawn on me that I was going through a kind of therapy. I was reliving my own experiences as a deaf child, and was, finally, finding, through the articles and booklets I wrote for Clarke Mainstream Services, the words to express what I had experienced when in the mainstream.

This work led to the opportunity to organize and offer workshops for deaf teens in mainstream schools. Quite a few of the kids who attended these workshops had never met another kid

With my Clarke Mainstream colleagues.

with hearing loss. With them I found the camaraderie I'd never known when I was their age. Equally important, when seeking out young adult role models for them to meet, I got to see what young deaf people are doing today. I was altogether thrilled to discover the confidence with which they are entering *every* profession, their commitment to helping others, and their comfort and ease with technology. And I saw how many of them had cochlear implants.

This, in turn, made me more aware of the children at Clarke Schools with cochlear implants. I couldn't help but notice how, in my classes, *they* were the ones who looked up right away and responded as I spoke. I didn't need to bang on the table top or flick the light switch to get their attention, or keep repeating what I'd said. I marveled too at the fluidity of the communications between them. Many can talk on cell phones and go to movies. Watching them I found myself thinking, "Hey, wait a minute, I want to go with you, I don't want to become a deaf dinosaur!"

And they beckoned to me to join them!

Wedding picture. April 6, 1968.

Ed and I have been married for over forty-five years. If you want to know what it's like for a hearing man to be married to a deaf woman, you will have to ask him. As for my take on it: he's wonderful and I am very, very lucky. And I don't think of myself as lucky *because* he's hearing, though he *has* made hundreds—maybe, by now, millions—of phone calls for me! I think of myself as lucky because we found each other, see eye to eye on all the important things, share many interests, and laugh often. I think *we* are lucky because I have heard it said that a large percentage of marriages between hearing and deaf people don't work. I can believe this, having seen up close how hearing loss, especially later in life, can cut two people off from one another in unexpected and tragic ways.

What I'm getting to here are *our* children, Ed's and mine. For even more important than the children I have taught have been our daughters. Teaching can be hard but parenting is surely the hardest job in the world. I say this because you open your heart in a very special way to another human being when you become a parent. I know now why my mother sought out the faith healer in Morocco *and* why my father wanted to protect my

Ed and I in 2001.

brother and me from the eye of the man with leprosy. Likewise I understand why my mother called me on my bluffing, kept after me in speech practice, and pushed me to be more social.

For me the most pressing question when we were expecting our first daughter was "How am I going to hear the baby?" I didn't want to depend on Ed's ears all the time. After all he wouldn't be nursing the infant, so why should we both have to

With Laurel, our first born, in 1972.

get up at night? Later I learned there are flashing light systems and bed vibrators to wake deaf parents in this sort of situation but doubt I would have tried them. I did not want a circus starting up every time the baby cried.

Laurel cried from 9 p.m. till 5:30 a.m. her first night at home. She looked red and raw. Neither of us got any sleep. We had observed Laurel sleeping blissfully in the arms of a nurse in the maternity ward of the hospital. Ed tried to reach her by phone and was told, in effect, "Sorry—we can't connect you with her, you're on your own."

We had no choice but to learn, and learn we did. Help came in the form of advice from other parents at the school where Ed taught at that time. Then, in the first week, I became aware of a hot, tingly sensation in the palms of my hands and up my arms whenever Laurel cried or was about to cry. This heat would wake me instantly at night, before Ed detected anything, and could even be felt when I was a couple of miles away from the baby. It was 100 percent accurate and continued for six to eight weeks. Three years later it returned when our second daughter, Christa, was born, and it lasted for roughly the same length of time.

BABIES BROKE ME OPEN

Babies broke me open
to mother sounds:
underarms sizzling hot,
telling me I was needed
even from afar,
faster than the telephone,
making the heart rear up
and the milk let down
as I hurried home,
gave myself up to the call
of the open mouth
demanding all,
latching on,
sucking with abandon,
while tiny fingers
floated in the air
conducting an ensemble
I could barely hear,
Eyes answering a smile
I could not see.

The family.

There really, truly *are* other ways of hearing when the ears don't work. In addition, both girls learned spontaneously when they were very young to look at me when they spoke, wanted my attention, or heard unusual sounds. I remember Laurel as a three-year-old taking my face between her two hands when I was talking with someone else, and turning it so I could see she was telling me she needed to go to the bathroom. And I remember Christa around the same age waking me one night to let me know the dog was vomiting! Both girls kept me informed in public when strangers were speaking to me—they still do—and they made and took many phone calls for me. I also remember both girls, in the imitative stage, pretending they, too, had hearing aids and walking around with heads tilted to hold hearing-aid batteries in their ears.

In addition, both girls have always been aware of my speechreading needs when in family or social situations—aware

Christa and Laurel.

in ways my parents never were, and able, when necessary, to communicate silently with me by way of speechreading across the room. They also know when I'm bluffing—they see right through it—and will kid me with, "You didn't get that! We know because you're wearing your Prize Day smile!"

I am able to communicate at a distance quickly with our daughters by email—and, for the first time, in advance of their father! I'm immensely grateful they try to make direct contact with me when they have big news to share—unlike other family members, who talk to Ed, knowing he will pass the information, or the gist of the conversation, on to me. For most of my life this was the case—in fact, it still is—even though people know I use email and have a TTY, a text telephone. It has bothered me at times. But our girls are different. They know me pretty well, and I feel fortunate to have not only two wonderful daughters, but two kind, wise, altogether delightful friends!

TO LAUREL AND CHRISTA

Is there, for you,
"Before" and "After"?

"She was deaf,
now she's less deaf."

"She was my mother,
now she's this bionic woman."

Let me know
what you decide.

As for me—
all these years,

the how of hearing
hardly mattered,

for it's always been
heart to heart.

Deafness has meant
bumps on the road,

reason to drive
slowly—or maybe faster—

look ahead,
plan, plot, press onward,

marvel at the scenery,
laugh a lot.

Our family in D.C. in 2009.

And now—oh joy—there are grandchildren!

Though I was eager and excited to see our daughters and their husbands become parents—and they've become wonderful parents—when Laurel was expecting, I experienced anew a certain apprehension. It was not the apprehension of "How will I hear the baby?" but rather "How will I understand the child?" Some of the apprehension came from listening to the stories of other grandparents. Not only grandparents who are late-deafened, but grandparents with normal hearing who have told me they can't understand their grandchildren when they talk. For some it had to do with the child's speech being intelligible, with others it had to do with the child's thoughts being incomprehensible. There were occasions too when it sounded to me as though these children had not been shown *how* to talk with their grandparents. There was little or no face-to-face contact, and some children exhibited outright impatience with the slower pace of their elders.

Having had good relationships with both of my grandmothers, I found such stories sad. I need not have worried, for Laurel has, all along, wanted what I want. So it has happened, *is* happening, and as I found out right at the start, I still hear pretty well with my eyes.

TO ELLIE, WHO CAME FIRST

Before my surgery
the ladies at work said,
"It's going to be wonderful
when you hear your granddaughter!"

As if I couldn't hear you already!

From the moment we met
you've been a clear, high note
in my innermost ear.

And your cry:
any deaf person
could get that!

Now—
I *am* filled with wonder
as I catch
the flit of your voice,
for it fits the flit of your fingers,
the circles you shape in the air with your arms,
the skip-hop-skip of your verve,
always on toes!

With Freya in 2011, the year I got the implant.

Six months after surgery for the cochlear implant, our second grandchild was born, and I was able, for the first time, to hear up-close, full-blast, the noises our children must've made when they were infants!

Three generations 2013.

Freya at Two Weeks

What I hear in your wail
is raw need:
food,
warmth,
coolness,
dryness,
reassurance,
closeness,
the sound
of your parents' voices
guiding you
into this world.

Before closing this chapter, I want, as a glad grandmother, to share with you another moment. Please understand what when I speak of "hearing" in the poem that follows I don't necessarily mean perfect physical hearing, I mean hearing as the ability to connect with other human beings.

Freya at Eight Weeks

Holding you,
rocking you,
singing to you,
all alone,
you and me,
your eyes on mine,
your eyes *in* mine,
without a blink,
or a burp,
or a pause,
or a yawn,
light, blue,
deep, warm,
joy rising up in me
higher, higher,
even into tears,
because I see you
on your way here
into our world,
because I see
you can hear!

Birds

WHEN I FIRST thought about the things I hoped to hear well, or better, with the cochlear implant, "everyday conversation" was at the top of my list. Then "children." Then came "birds." So now I'll tell you about the joy *and* the irritation of being able to hear birds again after sixty-two years. "Irritation?" you might wonder. Yes! And I'm *not* talking about the cawing of crows.

The crow *was* the first bird I heard in the winter of the year I got my implant. Next was the chickadee, and that, when Ed told me what I was hearing, was special. Because to my eye and ear, the *chickadeedee* call fit perfectly with the undulating flight pattern of the bird, in the same way and at the same time I was matching human voices with faces.

The chickadee was as far as I had gotten when it came to identifying bird calls, when spring breezed in during my first year with the implant. Then, overnight, I became aware of an explosion of exclamations outside. (That I could, when indoors, hear so many sounds coming from outdoors was also something very new for me. Later I also became aware of the metallic drone of crickets. To be honest, I did not, and still do not, find that an altogether pleasurable sound.)

To my ear it was as though *every* single bird around our house was proclaiming its existence. No bird waited for another bird to speak first, they all had to talk at once!

At first I was delighted:

As I hear one bird
everything begins
to sound like bird
calling from over there
out of sunlight,
unfurling leaves,
rounded bush squatting
in meadow nest,
calling,
calling,
to let the world know.
"I am here!"

In the morning after putting the implant on, I asked Ed if he could sort through these bird noises. I could hear the racket but didn't know how to interpret it. Could Ed tell by ear if he was hearing courtship, home defense, parental correction, or what? I wanted to be in on the news of the bird world, and Ed translated as best as he could with, "It sounds as though one bird over there (pointing out the window)—I don't know what kind it is—is calling, and a response is coming from other here." (More pointing.) Or, "It's just a lot of chatter, a lot of gibberish, right now." What he described was a heck of a lot more upbeat than the newspaper headlines!

However, when I sat down to work, the racket continued. Much of it came from the spruce outside the window of my writing room. I wished I could turn it off or turn it down the way Ed did with the radio. I figured the birds would calm down during the course of the day, but they didn't. On and on they went like wound-up toys. Don't birds get sore throats?

I tried ignoring them, but the calls came so regularly and were so persistent I felt as though I was unable to *not* listen for them. That, in turn, made it hard, if not impossible, to write. I knew I could turn the implant off, but I didn't want to. I *wanted* to be able to hear all the things I was hearing, from household sounds to my fingers on the keyboard to cars passing by on the road. It was strange realizing that I now felt *entitled* to these sounds after years of being without them. And I was hungry for more. Much more. I didn't want to go back into the silence except when *I* wanted to.

I began leaning out the window periodically shouting, "Be quiet!" That didn't help for long. Closing the window was no help either. The outdoor sounds had, literally, invaded my normally quiet indoor writing room! To top it off, when I took a break from my desk to do housework, or to walk, or garden, there were the same darn sounds. On and on and on. It was as though birds were following me everywhere!

I finally decided I should try to accept what I was hearing rather than seeking to escape or fight it. After all, why was I fussing about birds when I have always loved them? Hadn't I wanted to *be* a bird when I was six? Hadn't Ed given me a bird when we got married, and hadn't we had numerous wonderful bird pets over the years, from a troupial, to a canary, to a cockatiel, to a pair of finches? Though the pitch and regularity of these calls rubbed me all wrong, birds aren't machines. They were expressing something of profound importance to them. What was it?

For a set amount of time every morning, maybe ten minutes in length, I sat and listened to bird talk and let go of the need to do my work and get it done. I began to hear slight variations within their calls. I began, too, to look for the birds when I was outside. Which one lived in the spruce? Was I mostly hearing a he or a she? If he and she were conversing, what was the range of their wireless bird phone connection? Was one sending out a grocery list to the other? Was the other sending back reports on the availability of different items on the list?

It probably sounds as though I was anthropomorphizing the situation. It would've been wonderful to discuss the matter with a birder, but I didn't know of one close by, and I wasn't out to become one myself. I just wanted to find a way to move beyond the irritation. I just know I work better, and am a happier, kinder person when I feel in accord with the world around me.

I still don't know much more about birds and their varying calls, but I do know I can choose how I respond to sounds that bother me. The person with normal hearing develops a filter that blocks out bothersome sounds that may be repetitive, loud, harsh, or offensive. This desensitizing may be more necessary for some than for others. Think of people who live beside rail-road tracks where trains roar past periodically throughout the day and night. Along these lines, those who experience hearing loss later in life may have to readjust or rebuild these filters that have gradually, without their knowing, been dismantled as their hearing declined. I am still in the process of developing my own filters, and it will likely take me longer than it would take a child to get beyond the point of being distracted by a bush-full of chattering birds. I do this by acknowledging both the sound and my reaction to it, then turning my attention away from the sound to something else. The "something else" is usually something I like to look at: a plant, a color, even a cloud in the sky. Or I might talk with whomever I am with. When I become engrossed in whatever I have turned my attention to, I forget the birds and I no longer hear them. For hearing people this is, very likely, automatic, a no-brainer. For me, it's work. I also certainly do *not* want to become altogether unresponsive to bird voices, for, when I listen to them I can't help but feel deep appreciation for them. What insistence! What life and vitality!

The irritation I experienced in response to bird sounds during my first spring and summer with the implant brought home to me again and again how the cochlear implant really places me *in* sound. There are no boundaries in this hearing, except those I erect myself, either by turning the processor down, building up the inner filter, deliberately shifting my attention elsewhere as just described, or turning the processor off.

I also realized that I had brought certain expectations to hearing with the implant. I expected to like bird sounds and was surprised to discover otherwise. Not being tolerant of the rumble and roar of road construction outside my window was obvious. But birds? When I thought further about this expectation, it occurred to me I was expecting sweetness, melody, tunefulness. In short: composition. Composition implies order. As if all birds could, or should, sing in harmony! Instead, their voices sound all over the place, with no clear beginning, middle, or end to what they have to say.

The advancing season, that first year with the implant, brought the full boil of spring bird sounds down to a quieter summer simmer. Maybe I was imagining it, or maybe I was getting used to it, but their voices were, to my ear, less loud and urgent in August than they were in May. Then, as suddenly as these sounds burst into my awareness, they receded. I didn't miss them, but I did, quite ironically, look forward to hearing them when spring came around again. I wanted to see if they affected me the way they had when the implant was brand new. They *did* irritate me and still do, at times. Ed just grins when I say, "If *only* that bird would be quiet for a few minutes so I can hear what you're saying!"

And the crows? I often hear their cawing from inside the house when the windows are open. I find their comments and proclamations loud, insistent, and coarse, but they don't irritate me. It's crossed my mind—like the time when I was out walking, heard abrupt, wild cawing, and, moments later, a bear lumbered across the road up ahead—that the crows are self-appointed custodians commenting every now and then on activity below or in the trees. So, if I'm outside and they start cawing, I listen, and look around to see if they are trying to point out something important, for I'm not particularly eager to bump into a bear!

Music

I HAD EXPECTED to like bird voices and was surprised to discover they could irritate me. Meanwhile, family, friends, and total strangers expected, and still expect, me to be thrilled to hear music and are surprised when I tell them I don't hear music very well with the cochlear implant. When discussing the implant with the doctor before surgery, I was asked which of two types of implants I wanted to get. He described one as being geared toward clearer reception of music and the other as being better for those who want to hear human speech. I didn't hesitate to ask for the latter. Hearing people more fully, clearly, and quickly—my family especially—was at the top of the list of what I wanted. That the makers of cochlear implants address the fact that different parts of the brain are attuned to picking up and hearing different sounds, or so-called languages (researchers and medical professionals in the field of otolaryngology speak of the "Language of Music") was news to me. Perhaps someday there will be a cochlear implant with an app attuned specifically to Bird Language! This goes to show how very complex the act of hearing is, and what I'm sharing here with you is only a small portion of what waits to be discovered in the realm of hearing. For those who want to know more about the cochlear implant and music, go to Jeanne Coburn's chapter in the back of this book, as she speaks of this briefly there.

I had few expectations about being able to hear music when I got the implant. In addition, it had always irked me, when I wore a hearing aid, that hearing people assumed I couldn't hear music. Before I got The Brick I often, as a child, crawled down under the grand piano in our living room when my mother was playing and put my feet up on the black underbelly of the instrument. I loved listening to it that way, and I would often, when no one else was in the house, sit before the keys, close my eyes, and hope hard that when I opened them I would be able to play like my mother. Though I did learn "Chopsticks," I couldn't get beyond that—my hands did not flow up and down the keyboard the way hers did.

Then, at age fifty, I decided it was time to try to turn my piano-playing dream into a reality, and I took lessons with a vivacious Russian lady. Elena, and later Eveline, another brilliant teacher, tried, like the speech therapist I'd had as a child, to help me hear piano music by way of my other senses. They spoke of the notes as colors, from primary to secondary, from light to dark, and emphasized how the touch of the fingers could, and should, vary, from assertive and fast, to modest and slow, to merely suggestive, depending on what I was playing. Considering these different pressures helped me to hear each piece in my head as I learned to read music a bit. I knew I *had* to be able to hear the music in this way—within myself—in the same way that I *have* to hear written words in books before I can put them together in sentences and understand their meaning. Both piano teachers would make notations on the piece to help me remember the different parts and how they fit together. ("Light to dark—soft to heavy," and so on.)

For a while I dared hope my fingers could learn to know when I hit the wrong keys, since I couldn't hear those mistakes with my hearing aid, Likewise I dared to hope I could remember not only the music but my teacher's notations. I was inspired too by the example of the Scottish deaf percussion-ist, Evelyn Glennie. I love the thought of deaf people mak-ing music! However, though I may come back to the piano at some point now that I have a cochlear implant, my work with deaf children at that time kept me from regular practice at the piano, and I finally stopped altogether when I realized that pursuing music in this way was more drudgery than pleasure. Coming to this realization helped me begin to make peace with the words that had hovered over me when I was growing up: "You just have to try harder . . ." Sometimes we *do* "just have to try harder" in order to have a breakthrough and get where we need to go. Other times it doesn't make sense—either literally or figuratively.

In elementary school I dreaded music class and bluffed when singing by moving my lips as others moved theirs, rather than singing aloud and risking being totally out of tune. I did, as mentioned earlier, love ballet as long as I could see and fol-low what the teacher and the other dancers were doing. In this way I heard through imitation. And I loved—and still love—dancing, both country dancing and dancing with a partner, provided my partner can show me the beat, through tapping of the foot on the floor or fingers on my shoulder, as well as how the steps go. Again, the interweaving of the activities of our senses is evident, hinted at in the language just used. For I just spoke of my dance partner "showing" me how the steps go and how "hearing" these steps has as much to do with the sense of touch as it has to do with seeing, or hearing by way of a form of hearing aid.

Beat is the easiest, most accessible, means for me to find my way into music. Drumming or marching tunes can pull me right into an activity in which they are employed. It was also the beat I was listening for when I was under the grand piano, or when I put my hands on the radio, or attended concerts with The Brick or, later, digital aids turned as high as they would go. Likewise, there is heartbeat, windshield-wiper beat, the beat of waves breaking on a beach, the beat of 1-2-3 hand squeezes that mean "I love you," the beat of the tennis ball in a long steady rally or when playing against a wall. And more. It was a small step for me from hearing these obvious beats through hands, feet, and skin, to hearing beats within myself. Other deaf people have told me they, also, hear music within themselves. In the past, when I spoke of hearing music within, hearing people assumed I was remembering music I'd heard before I lost my hearing. But I doubt that, because these beats that I called music did not call up any memory of place or time, nor could I say they had a definite shape (beginning, middle, and end), and they varied greatly. They were always pleasurable, whether they were slow, fast, spirited, solemn, ongoing, or very brief—like musical haiku. In addition, I could not summon them the way one might summon a memory, or turn them on or off at will. They came and went and still come and go when I'm not wearing the implant. Maybe this so-called music is a kind of inner, emotional doodling. Maybe I'm picking up on the sound track of life. Maybe it's what mystics call the Music of the Spheres, and anyone, with or without normal physical hearing, may unexpectedly dip, or be dipped, into a fragment of it every now and then. As the blind speak of seeing within, so do the deaf speak of hearing within. Just because people with normal hearing can't see or hear what the blind and deaf see and hear within themselves doesn't mean those sensory impressions don't exist. After all, Beethoven, who knew deafness, heard within and found ways to share what he heard with the world.

Tone and melody are the most difficult things for me to access in music. I actually didn't understand until I was in my twenties that volume and tone are two different things. Even as hearing people may think the deaf will "get" what they are saying if they speak louder, I thought I would "get" music better if the volume of what I heard was raised. But dancing closer to the band greatly decreased, rather than increased, my appreciation for rock and orchestra music. Sitting in the front row at concerts or at the opera did not help either, and was, in fact, jarring.

I discovered with time that the type of musical instrument and the number of instruments being used was key to my enjoyment. In the same way that deep voices are easier and more enjoyable for me, deep-toned instruments are easier and more enjoyable. Piano, banjo, cello, French horn, oboe, drum, to name a few. Except for the piano, I usually cannot, even with the cochlear implant, name the instrument I'm hearing without having to look and see which one it is. Likewise, the fewer the instruments, the easier it is for me to follow the music, in the same way that conversation with one person is easier to follow than conversation in a group.

The beginning of my understanding of music not merely as beat but as tone and melody is hard to pinpoint and to describe. And—yet again—I know what I'm getting when I speak of hearing music is likely only a fraction of what the person with normal hearing gets. The closest I can come to describing it is to say that I became aware of certain feelings music was calling up in me. Feelings I wasn't, before then, even aware existed. As though music is a hand that can reach out and pluck or touch strings or keys within *us* so we resound with what is being played! I tried to express this in a poem I wrote many

years before I got the implant. On this occasion Ed and I, not
yet married, had just stepped out into a warm, clear July evening after attending a performance of chamber music.

THE MUSIC PLAYED ON

After the concert
the music played on and on
in me.

I have heard it many times—
sounding in the soles of my feet,
vibrating up my legs,
expanding in my chest,
tingling in my throat,
circling round my head,
pouring out of the palms of my hands . . .

(There is so much the hearing
don't know about hearing,
as if it's all in the ears,
only in the ears.)

This time was different
for my love walked beside me,
holding my hand,
the summer stars
singing like never before,
the notes rising, swooping,
rippling, thrilling
all around us.

He didn't hear what I heard.
I had to rein my heart in,
breathe slow and even,
tell my toes not to dance,
for our two palms
not only held each other,
the lines in them
were being woven together.

What exactly are these feelings I'm talking about in relation to music? Love, obviously. Beauty, harmony, and wonder as well. But, mostly, discovery. When I'm able to hear into music, I feel I'm entering into other worlds. If you have seen the look of surprise and delight on the face of a toddler when tasting ice cream for the first time, you will know what I'm trying to express here. The toddler's face might say, "What *is* this? I want more!" The toddler is experiencing a whole range of things: sweetness, coldness, creaminess, vanilla, chocolate, whatever. The toddler may, from then on, year after year on into childhood, then adulthood, with unabated pleasure, want to reach for this experience of ice cream.

Of course, not all music is like eating ice cream, and maybe there are children who *don't* like ice cream, sorbet, or gelato for that matter, but this doesn't mean the element of discovery isn't present. Musicians have told me that what is pleasurable in music varies from culture to culture. What we think of as happy music may sound sad to someone in another country, and vice versa. When I used a hearing aid and was open to "tasting" music, I had to be extra attentive to what I was trying to hear. I *wanted* to hear what was important to Ed, I wanted to experience what he experienced when he listened to music, and was just about blown off my feet by the little bit I did get!

This is *not* to say this happened every time I tried to listen to music. Where we sat, what instruments were being used, the length and complexity of the piece, how awake and rested I was: all these things mattered, and still matter. Over the years Ed has forgone many concerts (movies and plays also) that he realized I likely wouldn't be able to follow, and has had to listen alone to the radio and recorded music he enjoys. He says this is no big deal, there are plenty of other things we do together, but I am forever grateful for his thoughtfulness. Deafness affects *everyone* who is related to the deaf person.

No wonder Ed was hopeful that the cochlear implant might expand my experience of music. A few months after the surgery we sat down one evening and he tried out a couple of his favorite recordings. I was distressed to realize they all sounded pretty much the same to me. That, in fact, describes what happens after I've listened to the best of my ability for fifteen minutes or more to most recorded music. The start may be interesting, but then everything begins to sound the same. Not quite as bad as the "soup," the auditory chaos I experienced when I first got the implant, but it's still blurred and pervasive enough not to be anywhere near delicious. One thing that can help greatly, however, is having a transcript on hand of the words being sung, listening specifically for them, and even trying to sing along with them. I have several favorite songs. In addition, the musicality of poetry is as important to me as the thoughts the poet is seeking to express.

Live performances are usually easier for me to hear with the implant. The first one I heard, about three months after my first mapping, was a bagpipe recital by a neighbor. What I got sounded like loud, heavy, mooing noises! We left during the intermission, and I noticed, with some hilarity on the way out, that the wife of the bagpiper had been handing out earplugs!

Over a year later we attended a rehearsal of chamber music at the Marlboro Music festival in Marlboro, Vermont. A string quartet was working on a piece by Beethoven when we came in, and the little I heard went right into me. "What is this? I want more!" was exactly my response. Tears welled up in my eyes. It was as though Beethoven was talking *to* me. I listened as intently as I could for about thirty minutes and left feeling filled to overflowing. I believe the fact that the room was almost completely empty and the music could resound off the wooden surfaces may have helped me to hear as I did.

Since then I can remember two other occasions when, because of the cochlear implant, I was much moved by live music. One happened in a restaurant. We were having supper out with family, and as we came into the waiting space, I heard jazz being played across the room. The lightness and meandering nature of the pianist's touch caught my attention right away, making me want to get closer to the music. So I did what I'd done as a child: leaned against the piano (it was an upright) to listen by way of touch, and marveled not only at the beat but at the turning, winding, rambling "voice" of the notes. It was like taking a walk in a spring garden with commentary being offered first on this, then on that vine, and the flowers that came out of these tendrils.

Another occasion came at a choral concert by a small group of men and women who perform for people of all ages who are terminally ill or dying. The gentle harmony of the singing and the fact that I could hear and understand several of the refrains made a deep impression on me. At other choral concerts the singing had become overbearing "loudness" after I'd made an effort to listen for about half an hour. Turning the processor down did not help, and I couldn't take any more in and wanted to leave. By contrast, the music of this small group sounded like an invitation. It made me *want* to listen. It even made me want to try to sing along. And I did! What a contrast to my unhappy experiences in music class as a child!

When, after the performance, I tried to thank the director and tell him how it had been for me, he immediately offered to bring the group to our house to give a concert just for me.

"But I'm *not* dying," I said jokingly. "Sometimes the words 'deaf' and 'dead' get mixed up, as in the story of the man who called a taxi company to arrange a ride for his mother and warned them she was deaf. Then a hearse, rather than a taxi, appeared at the front door!"

What I didn't say then but will add now is: the music I am discovering because of the cochlear implant is far, far from death and dying. Being able to hear and enter into music feels like a birth—a longed-for and long-awaited birth.

More to Ponder

M Y EXPERIENCES WITH birds and with music got me thinking about quite a few other things, and other sounds as well, as you will see in the poems to come.

I've always found the philosophical question "If a tree falls in a forest and no one is around to hear it, does it make a sound?" a silly one. Silly because if I, for example, was standing in the forest at night in the dark without hearing aid or implant help and a tree came crashing down nearby I would, I'm pretty sure, hear it. I would hear it through my feet. And would likely be scared out of my wits!

It seems to me that movement, *any* form of movement, no matter how large or small, creates vibrations, and vibrations mean sound.

To follow the above train of thought a bit further: if a tree falls in a forest no person may be around to hear it, but don't other forms of life hear it? Like my friends, the chattering birds. What about bears, coyotes, mice, snakes, and insects? Don't their ears count? Is there a forest somewhere where there are *no* ears? For me, the more interesting question is not whether sound can exist without ears but how sounds differ for every being that has ears. The movements—the vibrations—you're accustomed to hearing, and the movements an animal is accustomed to hearing must be very different.

I cannot believe
what I hear

now in this room
with the open window
is everything—

creak of chair
click of pen
tear of paper.

I cannot believe
these are all
the dog at my feet hears,
or the birds
in the spruce by the window,
or you,
downstairs,
reading the paper.

Surely there are sounds within sounds,
sounds slithering
round in the air,
oozing out of the walls,
strumming down the sun's rays.

Maybe the dog gets them
but the birds don't,
little movements
only dogs hear.
Maybe the birds are attuned
only to the shift
of the eggs in the nest,
while you're hearing

the printed word
loud as the radio.

And I,
sitting here,
trying to learn to listen,
maybe I only hear,
truly hear,
what I open
my heart to.

One can't help but notice the personal perspective we bring to hearing. It happens all the time, everywhere. In our house Ed has always referred to this as "Deaf Power." Meaning the hearing aid previously, and the implant now, didn't and really don't, in the long run, have all that much to do with what I hear or don't hear. In other words, I hear what I *want* to hear and am deaf to what I *don't want* to hear. The teen who tunes out her mother's request that she clean her room, yet hears the first ring of the kitchen phone two floors down and gets to it in seconds is another example of this. Ed says I end, or interrupt, conversations by looking away from him. Okay, I'll admit I've done this. And I will clue you in on another Deaf Power move I sometimes use. A good time for me to make a point with Ed is when we're both in the car and *I'm* driving. If I'm talking, Ed can't—for the sake of our safety—interrupt, or add his two cents' worth, because I'll have to look away from the road, at him, to understand fully what he's saying. Very useful tactic!

Even as we bring our personal slant to hearing, we bring a personal slant to our experience of silence. Many people think deafness means silence. Silence as the complete absence of sound, an absence that can be anywhere from peaceful, to empty, to eerie and haunting. I, myself, have never known deafness as silence. Silence—true silence—is, for me, a rare and precious thing. A place of holy stillness, calm and light. A place to pause or rest and connect with the core of one's being.

Someone asked, "Don't you miss the silence?"

Deafness *is* the room removed
from the shrill edges,
blare, honk, shriek,
the ugly remarks
set loose to wound.

How much swearing have I been spared over the years?
How many decibels of thunder,
baby wail, crow protest, blender buzz,
backhoe boom-bang?

There *are* sounds that grate-irritate,
no question about that.
Do you want me to sound them?
I'll spare you!

And what are they beside the call of chickadee,
the way rain pitter-patters,
streammms, russsshes, drum-dum-dums,
the bubbly chatter-laughter
of children in a playground?

I *have* known the room removed,
deafness led me to it.
It isn't always quiet there.

Confusion is noisy, repetitive.
Excitement won't shut up.
Boredom is borrrrring.

No, deafness does not mean silence,
nor does hearing mean noise.

Then it occurred to me I might actually have it pretty good compared to hearing people. Because I can get away from bothersome sounds more quickly and completely than they. *But wait,* can I really, truly, get away from sound? Is there any place that is soundless? Outer sounds may be silenced when I turn the implant off, but then there are the inner sounds referred to in the last poem: the noisiness that accompanies confusion, the chatter of excitement, the static of boredom.

Can *you* choose
the level of sound
you're equal to
second by second?

I can—
four switches
from lowest to loudest,
softer to sharper,

up or down,
or when
enough is enough:
off!

Hamilton Relay Award. Spring 2011.

Ah! If only
inner sounds
could be picked and silenced
as simply.

Apart from pondering the nature of sound and sounds in a somewhat open, generalized way, I couldn't help but ponder the ways the implant was changing my daily communications with others. Was I becoming more of a "hearing" person because I was hearing more and better? Was I speechreading and face reading less as I heard more?

In response to the first question, I went through a phase of about six months when I felt myself to be less deaf because of the implant. The excitement of connecting to so many more sounds through the implant put me on a high.

In the past I had sometimes felt like a person in hiding. Let me explain this. Deafness has been spoken of as an "invisible" disability. The blind person can be detected by the cane, the uncertain walk, the seeing-eye dog. The person in the wheelchair is, obviously, unable to use his limbs in the same way as the person who can move freely. A behind-the-ear hearing aid can be obvious, but it also, for women specially, can be hidden by hair, scarf, or hat. For years I had worked to hide my hearing aid, because I wanted to slip by, rather than be stared at or singled out. It wasn't that I was ashamed of being deaf, I wanted to live like any person with normal hearing, participating in the activities of the hearing world. I didn't want extra attention, assistance, or pity.

There had been repercussions in my attempt to live in this way. Not only was this seen by some as a form of bluffing—some who were deaf, and were proud of being deaf, declared I was in denial. Why couldn't I embrace my deafness? They also—and this was quite painful—accused me of being a "Fake Deaf" person. Not only was I denying my deafness by trying to hide it from the world, I had not been born deaf, had not attended schools for the deaf, did not have deaf parents, and had married a hearing man. I was not the real thing, was definitely not one of them.

When I got the implant and began hearing so much more, I realized how divided I had felt at different times in my life. I had been brought up in the hearing world and considered myself a part of it, yet there was no getting away from deafness. I worked to be a better speechreader and to have clearer speech, but no matter how hard I worked, I never "arrived" in the hearing world, it was always beyond my reach. There was always the tantalizing "If you try a little harder, you *might* be able to hear."

Though people often said, "You've done a great job overcoming deafness," I cringed when I heard that. You can't "get over" being deaf, the way one gets over a cold or a broken leg.

Now, with the implant, not just more hearing, better hearing, but hearing "normally" suddenly felt closer. I hadn't been expecting or longing for this, likely because I couldn't remember what hearing had been like before I lost it. It just dawned on me little by little: "This is what it's like being able to hear all these little everyday sounds the way Ed, and others, hear them." It *was* exciting, no wonder I got high!

And it's *still* exciting! And I *still* get high as I make new discoveries! There are areas—music is foremost —that are to me like foreign countries I have yet to find my way into and explore by way of the implant. But the reminders that I am deaf remain: I *still* need closed captioning to get all the news, I *still* can't talk on the phone, I *still* can't understand the radio, and I *still* need to ask people to repeat. Put it another way: I *am* less deaf when I consider how much sound I am now taking in and making use of, but I will never *not* be deaf. This is not just a physical fact, deafness is not only my teacher, it's made me who I am. Saying I am no longer deaf would be as absurd as saying I am no longer an American.

As to the second question about speechreading and face reading less as I hear more, there are two answers.

Yes, I am speechreading less because, more and more, I hear and understand words without having to see the face of the person who is speaking. Such exchanges are usually quick, brief, passing. I will ask Ed from the kitchen if he's ready for supper, and I can hear his "yes" coming from the living room. Or I can hear my granddaughter say "bear" as she is running around the room, and I'll realize she's looking for her stuffed bear. Hearing little things in this way can be pretty exciting, and I have more to tell you about it in the next chapter.

The answer is also no, I am not speechreading or face reading less, because the need to see people full-face when I am conversing with them is so deeply ingrained in me. Being able to see the eyes particularly of the person I'm talking with makes for real, solid connection. When I can't see a person's eyes because they are looking elsewhere or because they are wearing dark sunglasses, I feel adrift. I still look across the room for silently spoken clues from Ed or our daughters when at parties. At meetings I still feel the need to sit where I can see the main speaker up close.

When word that I have a cochlear implant first spread among neighbors and people I knew around town but didn't talk with all that often, I could see by the way they looked at me how curious they were. Or they did a double take when they first noticed the implant on my head. In cases where it was obvious they wanted to ask about it but were shy about asking, I'd tell them. Then, next time I saw them they would want to hear about it all over again. In some instances it was as though we had never really connected till then. I am grateful for their interest. Sometimes when this happens, I wonder if I now, in some way, look less deaf to them. Sometimes, too, I remember awkward moments we had in the past when I knew they weren't exactly sure how to talk with me or if I would understand them, almost as though I was a person from a foreign country.

Meeting a Neighbor in Town

> "Yes, thank you,
> I can hear you.
> I can hear your voice."

No point in mentioning
I also hear your face
through my eyes,
your words lined up
like groceries
at the cash register.

Sugar in the greeting,
milk in the queries,
bread in the bits of news
we choose to share.

There's satisfaction
at getting through the checkout
without a mishap—
no spilt beans,
no weird uncomprehending looks,
no "Excuse me, what did you say?"
no meltdown
over the horrendous noise—
you probably don't notice—
in the background,
all the necessary items covered.

Alone again,
heading home,
giving myself over to the delicious
swish-swoosh-swish
of the summer breeze
fingering through my hair
and the hilarious

clankety-clink-clink-clack
of the car keys,
I try out my first yodel
as I pass your house.

One day I think, yes, my experience of deafness *is* different, very different, since I got the implant.

The next day I feel, no, it isn't all that different. Inside I'm the same person. And that's fine with me.

So—
I've been deaf
all these years.
No bird caw,
rain plash,
river rush,
wind rustle,
dog yowl,
voice twang.

Talk eddies
swirled past me
inches away
while I,
the fish
with unblinking eye,
flip-flopped
high
on the bank.

Can't say
it's all changed
overnight.
I'm still,
often,
shore bound,
watching,
waiting,
listening with all my being.

Bigger Steps Yet

As I trust I have made clear by now, from age six on, learning how to understand what people were saying was hard work. I had to pick up face reading and speechreading quickly, figure out the best circumstances for doing that, from being able to see people's faces, to realizing that light behind a person could obscure their mouths, to knowing if a person was sympathetic or impatient, and so on. This was exhausting work. You learn quickly who your real friends and allies are, who might offer help, and who doesn't care. You learn, too, there are times when retreat *is* necessary, regardless of what people think, and your health, physical and psychological, depends on getting enough sleep or shifting to another activity altogether.

For over sixty years, communicating with others has, for me, meant paying attention, watching faces and group dynamics closely, almost like a spy, while trying to collect additional clues through the hearing aid. Then, barely a month after getting the implant, something amazing and totally unexpected happened.

I was leaving a couple of Ed's shirts off at the cleaners and saw, as I came in, that the woman behind the counter was talking on her cell phone. Sometimes, for fun, I "listen in" on the conversations of others in public places by way of speechreading, but it seemed rude at that moment, so I averted my eyes, and a second later heard her say, "Someone came in. . . . Bye now."

I was certain I had heard her perfectly, without looking at her. Just for good measure I asked her what she had said, and walked out in a daze! And it kept happening. Not every day, and just about always when I least expected it. These moments of hearing and understanding perfectly what I was hearing without using my eyes at all were—and still are—like bright little birthday surprises tucked into the folds of each week.

Now and then
without any effort
I get a whole sentence!

"Have a nice day."
"It's time to go."
"I'll call you back later..."

I get shivers
hearing like this,
hearing like everyone else.

It's as though a bird
swooped down,
perched lightly on my hand.

At the Post Office

Puffing up the stairs,
eyes on the ground,
heavy package in my arms—

"How're you doing?"
The words come to me—
near, clear, loud.

Startled I look up,
glance back, see a grin,
a wave, a thumbs up.

No one I know.
Yet I heard him,
knew his words were *to me,*

got them,
acknowledged them,
did it all by ear!

I continue to experience this effortless hearing without need-ing to see the face of the person who is speaking. Sometimes when watching the news on TV, I'll get a sentence or two, then will read those same sentences in captioning, and think, "Hey, I already heard that!" (That the captioning is often a couple of sentences behind what the news reporter is saying is a perfect example of how the person with hearing loss is often a couple of words, or sentences, behind what's being said.) This does not mean, however, that I can manage without captioning, I'm still, to use the term introduced early on in this book, "brain deaf" to much that hearing people take in without a second thought. Or I'll catch a couple of words on the radio program Ed's listen-ing to, isolated words that don't necessarily clue me in to the topic of the program.

I don't know if I will ever be able to listen along with Ed to a baseball game on the radio, though I rather doubt it. Or talk on the telephone with our daughters, though I now *can* hear their voices coming out of the machine. (I haven't yet told them their phone voices sound high and scratchy!) The surgeon warned me at our first meeting when we discussed the implant not to get my hopes up in this department. He said it looked, from my audiogram, as though my loss was too great and had happened too long ago for it to be likely the implant would make a difference in these areas. But the surprise of the effortless hearing I've described makes me hopeful. I wonder too how I can assist it. One obvious way is to read along with someone. Ed and I do this: we'll sit opposite one another, each with a copy of the same book. I won't look at him, only at the book. Ed will read aloud and will suddenly stop reading midsentence. I will pick up where he stopped and read aloud from where he has left off. We shift back and forth this way. Maybe a day will come when I'll be able to sit, empty-handed, and just listen to Ed reading. At the moment I think it is a long way off.

Is the potential to hear, understand, and make use of speech in *every* brain regardless of the age of that person, whether they are deaf or not? My own guess, right now, is yes, it *is* there! We barely know what we're capable of!

I believe there are two crucial factors: our attitude and our attention. They are the source of our power when it comes to hearing and comprehending what we are hearing. Without them the brain is just a brain, and technology, no matter how advanced and refined, is just technology. In a nutshell: Is my attitude open, hopeful, expectant? And is my attention geared toward hearing, listening for, and understanding human speech? In short, are *all* my senses focused on speech? They have been throughout my life, not only in speechreading but also in reading and writing as well. I happen to be a word-oriented person. So, as the implant brings me the sounds that words are clothed in, every now and then *everything*—all I am taking in—clicks into place. When this happens, I truly come to my senses! I know the interweaving and overlapping of *all* my senses are working together. I find myself moving into and through the rainbow of communication.

To Sum Things Up

LOOKING BACK

I see myself bluffing,
wanting to slip by undetected,
wanting to look like everyone else.

Sometimes I bluffed
because I assumed I couldn't get what was being said.
Truth is, many times I *couldn't* get it
no matter how good my lipreading skills,
and the can't-get-its can add up,
become the habit of giving up.

Yet bluffing also forced me
to "get it" some other way.
You don't hear only through
those funny flaps on the sides of your head.

I developed the necessary radar
for detecting kind-hearted souls
quick to clue me in, explain the situation,
repeat the joke, take notes,
without a shred of pity.

And I learned to "get it"
by picking up what spoken words omit:

137

how the lines around the mouth
can give away a lie
while the eyes play innocent.
How the hands can tell
if a person's generous or stingy.
How thoughts and feelings
sculpt every face:
sometimes lightly,
wind over sand,
often deeply,
water over rock,
grave or aglow,
always meticulously.

LOOKING AT NOW

I see an evolving need.

Who's speaking?
What's happening?
Where's all this noise going?
Why does it have to be clamorous, insistent, *everywhere*?

Maybe I can't "get" what you're saying on the first try
or the second, or the third . . .
but I *hear* those words,
they're alive,
they're powers!

Before:
colors, forms, gestures, faces

called up tones within:
red often shouts,
blue can whistle,
trees whisper,
rocks snore,
faces can shift within a sentence
from loud to soft,
to loud again.

Now it works the other way too—
noises, sounds, tones,
have colors, forms, gestures,
faces to explore.

I've landed in a smorgasbord!

I want to sing
rather than mouthing words,
meet jazz, classical, hip-hop,
get acquainted with the talk of leaves
in storm or breeze,
learn to say, "Hey, I'm here!"
when I don't get it.

Yes, hello, vast world of sound!
I've become the bird in the spruce
outside the window,
the bird proclaiming,
"I am here!"

Three years have passed since I got my cochlear implant. Though I am writing less frequently about it in my journal, and mostly in prose, the journey continues. Last week, for example, I was able to identify the strange sound I sometimes hear when going up the stairs in our house. It was the sound of the metal of my ring knocking against the wooden banister. I now remember this sound. I know it happens when I use the banister, and I know I make other sounds too when I do certain things. So I am learning to move through the world in new ways. For instance, when I'm taking dishes and flatware out in the early morning in preparation for breakfast. Do I want to do it quietly and let Ed sleep, or do I want to do it with the bang and clatter I now know I made before the implant, and wake him up? Ha! Sometimes it is tempting to make loud statements!

I cannot, however, remember all the sounds I am getting. There are just too many. I have become desensitized to a large portion of the noises that seemed so astonishing when I began hearing them through the implant. Put another way, I am still learning to absorb and selectively sort through sounds, rather than being overwhelmed by them. But sometimes—when in a busy city, at a noisy party, or when Ed's using the lawn mower or chain saw nearby—I can get a little dizzy. When that happens, I turn the processor off or excuse and remove myself.

Speaking of dizziness, I've decided there is profound wisdom in the observation that the sense of hearing and the sense of balance are closely connected. Apart from the fact that the senses of position and bodily balance are connected to the fluid in the inner ear and vertigo can come on when this organ is upset, the ability to manage many sounds is quite clearly a balancing act. Furthermore, it seems to me the sheer number and variety of sounds one has to deal with is just one part of this balancing act. Gauging or simply accepting the placement, activity, and energy of all these sounds is another part of the balancing act.

To be more specific: when I first got the cochlear implant, I often felt as though sound was coming right *at* me. But, technically speaking, most of the sounds I heard were not coming right at me. Whistling kettle, screech of brakes, sudden boom of thunder—it's taken me three years to begin to get over jumping when I hear them. Perhaps I will always feel assaulted by sudden loud noises—I'm sure that's true for people with normal hearing too—but now I know sound is everywhere, background, foreground, all around, just about all the time. And not only do all things, like even my ring on the banister, have their own sound or sounds, the way all things have their own texture, size, weight, color, and so on, there are sounds within sounds. *We truly live in an ocean of sounds.*

I find this thought deeply reassuring, deeply communal, deeply balancing. When I was younger, I could see when people were communicating and often wondered what I'd missed. "Oh, that was nothing, he just said have a good day," I can remember my brother telling me one time after we'd gotten on the bus and I asked him what he'd been talking about with the bus driver. Now, because of the implant, I am much more attuned to the quick spoken exchanges, the pleasantries that are a part of the glue of everyday life in the same way that a glance, a nod, or a smile are a part of life.

People constantly want to know what I like hearing that I couldn't hear before with the hearing aid. I tell them about wind in the leaves, rivers and streams, waves lapping on the shore, the inflection of children's voices when they're playing happily together, the wonderful warmth in some voices, the welcome home howl our dog gives when we walk in the door, light jazz on the piano, and, yes, the chirping of some birds. The list is still growing!

My journey of hearing with the cochlear implant continues, though at a slower pace. When strangers ask if I recommend that they get one, I always pause. I pause because I don't know the type or degree of their hearing loss, how long they've had it, what they wish to hear, their circumstances at home or at work, the amount of time and energy they want to invest in learning to hear with an implant, and so on. I tell them getting a cochlear implant is a personal matter. And deafness is a personal matter too! To live well, happily, and productively, I have had to find and forge my own individual relationship with it. In the process it has shown me my mettle and made clear to me that relationships can *always* continue to evolve. There's another reason I got the cochlear implant.

Almost sixty-five years later, deafness still tells me, as it did when I was a child, to step out if I want to be part of the world, rather than waiting for it to come to me. It reminds me that bluffing isolates and hurts *me* more than anyone else. It tells me to observe people carefully, for they speak in *many* ways, not just through their mouths, and there's *so* much right there, waiting to be found, when one looks beyond outer appearances. Deafness shows me how solitude is quite different from loneliness and how, in solitude, one can find both an inner voice of faith as well as one's outer voice. Above all, deafness reminds me, though I may feel whole and altogether intact in the center of myself, I am *always* vulnerable. Vulnerable to mistakes, miscommunications, misunderstandings. So, though I got a cochlear implant, am hearing more and more, and am eager to hear yet more and more, I am still vulnerable. But aren't we all? Deaf or hearing, we can choose how we respond.

Again,
and yet again,
and again,
I will say "Yes"—

Yes, hello, vast world of sound!
I've become the bird in the spruce
outside the window,
the bird proclaiming,
"I am here!"

Acknowledgments

Enormous thanks

to

my parents.

To the scientists, physicians, and audiologists
who have given us the cochlear implant.
And especially to Theodore Mason and Jeanne Coburn
who gave me *my* cochlear implant!

To the clinical trial patients willing to be guinea pigs
in the early stages of this amazing technology.

To the deaf children and young adults
who dared me to give it a go.

To my friends from Clarke Mainstream Services.

To our daughters, Laurel and Christa, my brother, John,
and other family and friends who have the patience,
take the time, and give so much
to experience deafness from the outside in.

Last, but really first, this book is for
Edward,
my home base in the hearing world.

Appendix

An Audiologist Explains the Cochlear Implant
Jeanne Coburn, Au.D.

I believe my very first cochlear implant recipient best summed up the impact of getting a cochlear implant: "It's the closest thing to a miracle that I've ever experienced." The technology is truly incredible, and many cochlear implant recipients are able to hear sound and understand speech amazingly well, but it's not the same as normal hearing. It has been a blessing to be able to work with cochlear implants over the last ten years and share the lives of over 250 individuals as they underwent this transformative procedure.

As an audiologist, I explain cochlear implants to potential cochlear implant recipients and their families. I will try to walk you through the process that they experience.

Qualifying for an Implant

There are many aspects of cochlear implant candidacy, including a person's medical history and current medical status, hearing history, age of onset of hearing loss, duration of deafness, use of hearing aids, psychological readiness, support of family and friends, and their understanding of realistic expectations for the process and possible outcomes for how they will hear with the implant. Some patients have already seen the cochlear im-

---

Dr. Coburn is board certified in audiology with a specialty in cochlear implants.

plant surgeon and may have an idea of whether or not they are a candidate. Others are referred by their audiologist, primary care physician, family members, or friends.

Often, I am the first stop in the cochlear implant candidacy process. Many potential candidates have some degree of nervousness about learning the results of their cochlear implant evaluation, which includes a regular hearing test in the sound booth while wearing headphones as well as special testing while using their hearing aids. A typical cochlear implant candidate has severe to profound hearing loss and no longer receives (or never did receive) sufficient benefit from hearing aids during their daily life. Technically, "insufficient benefit," as defined by the FDA, means that an adult candidate scored below 60 percent when repeating sentences heard while wearing one or two hearing aids. In everyday life, insufficient benefit means that a person is no longer or never was able to understand speech when listening on the telephone, when someone is talking from a distance, or when the person talking is not facing the listener. In general, for cochlear implant candidates, understanding daily conversation through listening alone is a struggle. Many rely on their vision for speechreading to supplement their hearing in understanding spoken language. Some patients with profound hearing loss come to my office with only a whiteboard and marker or pen and paper as their mode of communication.

How the Implant Works

A cochlear implant is composed of an internal device, which is the actual "implant," and an external device called the sound processor. The sound processor sits behind the recipient's ear and looks like a large hearing aid. The processor has a short wire coming off it that connects to a small round disc called

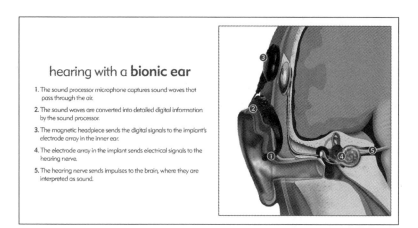

Figure 1. How a cochlear implant works. Courtesy of Med-El.

the headpiece or transmitting coil. The headpiece has a magnet in it. The magnet is used to hold the circular headpiece onto the scalp in the correct position over the internal device. The sound processor has one or more microphones that pick up the sound. The sound is then transmitted to a computer chip that codes the sound for the internal device. The coded sound travels down a short wire to the headpiece with the magnet and then is transmitted to the internal device (see figure 1).

The actual cochlear implant has a receiver/stimulator component implanted underneath the scalp behind and slightly above the ear. An electrode array with 16 to 22 electrodes comes out of the receiver/stimulator and is surgically placed into the cochlea. The receiver/stimulator is composed of a magnet, an antenna, and a computer chip. The internal implant receives the sound coded by the processor and transmits the coded sound and the necessary power to the electrode array in the cochlea. The electrode array directly stimulates the auditory nerve, which then conducts the signal up to the brain for decoding into sound.

The cochlea has truly magnificent architecture. It is a long tube coiled up into a snail-shaped structure that takes two and a half turns. It is lined with thousands of hair cells that convey sound vibrations to the auditory nerve. Sound travels into the cochlea as a vibration and then is transformed into an electrical signal that the brain can interpret via the stimulation of the hair cells and auditory nerve. What is especially remarkable about the cochlea is its tonotopical layout, meaning different tone frequencies are transmitted separately along specific parts of the structure. The basal end or base of the cochlea transmits the high-frequency (pitch) sounds. The frequency of the sound gets progressively lower toward the deepest bass sounds as the cochlea turns toward the apex. The tonotopical layout of the cochlea is what allows the cochlear implant to work as well as it does. Each electrode of the cochlear implant is assigned a range of frequencies to transmit to the auditory nerve, with the higher pitches in the base and the lower pitches toward the apex of the cochlea.

Cochlear implant candidates experience a variety of emotions, including interest, trepidation, fear, relief, sadness, and hope, when they learn that they qualify for the surgery. While grappling with their emotions, they also have to learn about the three cochlear implant manufacturers—Advanced Bionics, Cochlear Americas, and Med-El—and the types of devices available on today's market. They also learn general information about the surgery, how the cochlear implant works, and what they might experience while getting used to hearing through a cochlear implant.

During the counseling process, patients are able to look at all three cochlear implant systems, including the internal and external components. They are provided with manufacturer literature and can choose the device they receive. All three manufacturers have similar outcomes for speech understanding. Music usually produces more complicated sounds than speech, as it often incorporates a vocal component (singing) merged with an instrumental component. I counsel my patients that cochlear implants were designed primarily for understanding speech and that music appreciation can be challenging.

Activation and Mapping of the Implant

At our cochlear implant center, the surgery takes about two hours and patients go home the same day. When the patient wakes up from the surgery they will have a tight wrap around their head that comes off after twenty-four hours and they can take a shower and wash their hair after forty-eight hours. All stitches are self-dissolving and under the skin, so that there are no stitches or staples to take out later.

Initial activation of the cochlear implant takes place about seven days after surgery. This is the day that the cochlear implant recipient first hears sound through the implant. It's a very exciting and emotional day for all involved, often with smiles and tears of joy and happiness. Patients usually bring their family members to this appointment so that they can share the experience, and I've often joked that I'll need a stadium to include everyone who is interested. It is an honor for me to be part of this important moment in each implant recipient's life, and I have often been moved to tears by the amazed response of the patients and their families.

Adjustment of a cochlear implant is called mapping or programming. During a mapping appointment, the audiologist works with the cochlear implant recipient to determine the least amount of electrical current needed to create a sensation of hearing on individual electrodes. This is called a threshold, or T level. They also work together to determine the amount of current that generates a maximum amount of loudness that remains comfortable on individual electrodes, called an M (for most comfortable) or a C (comfortable) level, depending on the manufacturer. Those parameters create the "map" for each recipient's cochlear implant. Every recipient has her own "map" that optimizes her hearing through the cochlear implant. During the first three months of listening through a cochlear implant, most patients will return for map adjustments five or six times because their ability to tolerate the electrical stimulation increases over time. As times passes, the adjustments needed become smaller and so most return another three or four times during the remaining first year of cochlear implant use. Recipients will continue to come for adjustments once or twice a year for the remainder of their lives in order to ensure that the cochlear implant system is functioning properly and that the settings remain optimal.

When the author of this book, Claire Blatchford, chose to receive a cochlear implant, she took a big leap of faith. I say this not because there was a risk that the technology wouldn't work for her, because cochlear implants are very reliable, but because she had only one ear that she was used to listening with. It is a big step to "trade" the hearing you are familiar with for hearing through a cochlear implant. For most of her life, Claire has used a hearing aid on her right ear only. This meant that only the right ear was a good candidate for cochlear implantation. Her left ear was not a candidate for hearing aid use or cochlear implantation. Claire was therefore not able to listen via a left hearing aid while she was getting used to the cochlear implant, as many other patients do. When Claire was using her right hearing aid, she was able to hear sound within the range of moderate hearing loss (40–60dBHL) in the low pitches and was unable to hear any high-pitched sounds. In daily conversation, she was able to hear the vowels and some of the lower-pitched consonants such as w, r, n, and m, but she could not hear the softer, higher-pitched consonants such as s, f, t, p, k, and h. With her cochlear implant, Claire is able to hear sounds within the range of normal hearing for all the frequencies and hear all the sounds of speech. This level of hearing is common for a cochlear implant recipient. Being able to hear such soft sounds allows someone with a cochlear implant to hear amazingly soft sounds that most hearing people take for granted. Many of my patients have expressed joy and awe at being able to hear sounds such as rainfall, wind blowing, crickets, birdsong, foot-steps on creaking floors, the swish of ski jacket material, dog tags jingling, and leaves skittering across the ground. It does take time to learn to understand speech heard through a co-chlear implant, and the clarity of the speech varies from person to person. With her CI, Claire is able to understand familiar words and phrases and is also able to use the speech she hears to augment her speechreading skills.

As of December 2010, over 219,000 people worldwide have received cochlear implants. Of that 219,000, approximately 71,000 recipients were in the United States, 42,600 adults and 28,400 children. According to Blanchfield et al. (2001), as many as 738,000 individuals in the United States have severe to pro-found hearing loss. Of these, almost 8 percent are under the age of eighteen. Cochlear implants are a growing option for those with severe to profound hearing loss, and the technology con-tinues to improve at a rapid rate. The future holds great options for those with hearing loss.

For more information on cochlear implants, please refer to the following websites:

www.nidcd.nih.gov/health/hearing/pages/coch.aspx
www.advancedbionics.com
www.cochlear.com
www.medel.co

Further Reading

Books and Booklets by Claire H. Blatchford, published by Clarke Schools for Hearing and Speech

Exploring Careers: Adults with Hearing Loss in the Work Place, 2012.

101 Ways to Encourage Self-Advocacy in Children with Hearing Loss, 2010.

Summer Jobs and Beyond: A Guide for Teens with Hearing Loss, 2009.

What Works for Me: Young Adults with Hearing Loss Talk to Teens, 2005.

More Books by Claire H. Blatchford

Going with the Flow. Carolrhoda Books, 1998 (for children).

Nick's Secret. Lerner Publications, 2000 (for children).

Nick's Mission. Lerner Publications, 1994 (for children).

Many Ways of Hearing: 94 Multitasked Lessons in Listening. J. Weston Walch, 1997.

Full Face: A Correspondence about Becoming Deaf in Mid-Life. Butte Publications, 1997.

Biographies, Memoirs, Fiction, and Nonfiction about Deafness

Bouton, Katherine. *Shouting Won't Help: Why I—And 50 Million Other Americans—Can't Hear You.* Farrar, Straus and Giroux, 2013.

Chorost, Michael. *Rebuilt: How Becoming Part Computer Made Me More Human*. Houghton Mifflin, 2005.

Christiansen, John. *Reflections: My Life in the Deaf and Hearing Worlds*. Gallaudet University Press, 2010.

Cohen, Leah Hager. *Train Go Sorry: Inside a Deaf World*. Vintage Books, 1995.

Glennie, Evelyn. *Good Vibrations: My Autobiography*. Hutchinson, 1990.

Itani, Frances. *Deafening*. Grove Press, 2004.

Kisor, Henry. *What's That Pig Outdoors? A Memoir of Deafness*. Penguin Paperbacks, 1990.

Oliva, Gina. *Alone in the Mainstream: A Deaf Woman Remembers Public School*. Gallaudet University Press, 2004.

Rosner, Jennifer. *If a Tree Falls: A Family's Quest to Hear and Be Heard*. The Feminist Press at CUNY, 2010.

Swiller, Josh. *The Unheard: A Memoir of Deafness and Africa*. Holt Paperbacks, 2007.

Uhlberg, Myron. *Hands of My Father: A Hearing Boy, His Deaf Parents and the Language of Love*. Bantam, 2009.

Wright, David. *Deafness: An Autobiography*. HarperCollins, 1987.

Zazove, Philip. *When the Phone Rings, My Bed Shakes*. Gallaudet University Press, 1993.